The Rupture

On Knowledge and the Sublime

Words: Olivia Fane
Art: John B. Harris

imprint-academic.com

Published in the UK by
Imprint Academic Ltd., PO Box 200, Exeter EX5 5YX, UK

Distributed in the USA by
Ingram Book Company,
One Ingram Blvd., La Vergne, TN 37086, USA

ISBN 9781788360388

A CIP catalogue record for this book is available from the
British Library and US Library of Congress

Contents

The Other Shore

List of plates

All by John B. Harris, unless specified

The Other Shore

Introduction

What is the sublime?

The word 'sublime' comes directly from the Latin *sublimis* meaning 'exalted, high, lofty', and its first theorist, Longinus of the first century A.D., who wrote in Greek, uses the word *hupsos*, literally, 'Height', as his title. It's curious that Philip Shaw, in his book *The Sublime* (who has probably drawn on other commentators before him) prefers another etymology:

> Consider again the Latin roots of the sublime: *sub* (up to) and *limen* (lintel, literally the top piece of a door). Etymology itself suggests that there is no sense of the unbounded that does not make reference to the placing of a limit or threshold.[1]

In fact, 'sub' never means 'up to' and always means 'under', and it's curious that anyone ever saw any association with 'sublime' in its modern usage and a word meaning 'under the door lintel'. Nonetheless, such a strange etymology pleases those who wanted to see the sublime firmly bounded and within our control.

Mark Cheetham, whom Shaw quotes, argues that pleasure arises from the sublime in the 'framing' of a 'work' (in reference to Derrida's concept of a 'parergon' surrounding an 'ergon' and thereby defining it), and not in 'the glimmering awareness of something incommensurably "other"':

> The experience and pleasure of the sublime do not stem from the promise of something noumenal, outside a given frame, but rather from the perpetual, yet always provisional, activity of framing itself, from the *parergon*.[2]

In this essay, however, I want to suggest that the sublime as object is *never* bounded, but constitutes what is 'radically other'. Definitions, frames, etymology can throw no light on its meaning.

The sublime is the negative of all descriptions: infinite, unbounded, unknowable, ineffable, nameless. I shall follow Kant, but take his ideas even further, and suggest that it is known not by what it is or is not, but its function: namely to reveal ourselves to ourselves. The sublime is the whole package: noun and verb, being and doing. The sublime is the vehicle that transports us to knowledge and truth, and rejoices in their undecidability. The sublime as object is uncontainable, and will always reign supreme, unbounded. It is only the feeling engendered within us that we can 'frame' with any success.

I have found interesting allies among the post-modernists. Having established there is no 'hors-texte' – the meaning of a text depending on the interrelatedness of the words within it – Derrida positively cries out for 'tout autre', something which is real and other. John Caputo is another philosopher who plays with language rather than revering its truth claims, but his ambition to 'unmask' and thereby reveal is more reverent than destructive. He asks us the question: what do we really mean when we say that 'God' is love?

The troublemaker here is the word '*really*', which is attempting to 'unmask' the passion for love as a passion for God, or, alternately, to 'unmask' the passion for God as a passion for love.

> The first unmasking is pre-modern, theological … The latter unmasking is modernist, critical and desublimating … Either way, the unmasking claims to boil things down to the way they *really are*.[3]

Caputo's solution is to admit he does not know what is 'Really Real', in fact, no one does – 'unmasking' is not what it's cracked up to be – but he says, 'I have pledged my troth to the hyper-real.' Caputo declares: 'Religious truth is a truth without knowledge.'[4] When truth and knowledge are bedfellows, there is neither truth nor knowledge. The quest for certainty, to 'unmask', is doomed. But that does not mean that all we have left is chaos and meaninglessness:

We are not left with nothing, but with the passion and the not-knowing. The passion *of* not-knowing, truth without Knowledge, the restless heart.[5]

For Caputo, then, the 'hyper-real'; for me 'the sublime'. The 'passion of not knowing' is the very core of the encounter.

In my first chapter, I consider the primary texts on the sublime, by Longinus, Burke and Kant. In my second, I look at how 'what is radically other' is helpful in forming an epistemology which is more than merely analytic. I introduce my paradigm for this essay, Hilary Lawson's terms of 'Openness' and 'Closure', and suggest that by the very act of 'bounding' we thereby close but can share; whereas subjective openness is by its very nature solipsistic but nonetheless necessary for the acquisition of new knowledge. In my third and final chapter, I look at the relationship between the sublime, post-modernism and negative theology. I shall conclude by suggesting that an attitude of openness towards what we do not know, and of resisting closure, is a pathway not just to the sublime, but to truth itself.

Chapter One

The Literature

A philosophy of the sublime begins with its first exponent, Longinus of the first century, a writer little known until the seventeenth and eighteenth centuries, when he was read with renewed vigour by the poets and philosophers of the Enlightenment. He was read by and indeed influenced Burke, who in turn was read by Kant, and as Kant's theory of the sublime is the most sophisticated of the three it is to him that I shall turn most in formulating a working definition, or, more accurately, delineating the space which the sublime might occupy.

Longinus

Longinus himself was primarily concerned with literary criticism. Interestingly, he wrote at a time when Romans were anxious about plagiarizing Greek poets, which they did continually, and yet yearned to be original at the same time. In the eighteenth century the preoccupations of the cultural elite were much the same: they revered Classical literature and architecture, yet equally wished to put their own stamp on it.

Longinus equates sublimity with authenticity – the subject matter might be the same, but feeling must come fresh from the heart.

Longinus dispenses advice in the form of a letter addressed to a 'Postumius Terantianus':

> Sublimity is a kind of eminence or excellence of discourse. It is the source of the distinction of the very greatest poets and prose writers and the means by which they have given eternal life to their own fame. For grandeur produces ecstasy rather than persuasion in the hearer; and the combination of wonder and astonishment always proves superior to the merely persuasive and pleasant. This is because persuasion is on the whole something we can control, whereas amazement and wonder exert invincible power and force and get the better of every hearer.[6]

The significant words here, which will carry through to further descriptions of sublimity, are *grandeur, ecstasy, wonder* and *astonishment*; and the significant concept is that of *being in the power of something other*: what is happening is *beyond our control*.

We don't go out in search of the sublime; rather it is the sublime that seizes us. The Greek word for ecstasy is *ecstasis* and literally means, 'standing outside ourselves'. The Romantic response to the ideas and logic of the Enlightenment was to *remove* man from the centre of his Universe and to set him at the mercy of it all over again. But in both Longinus' time and the eighteenth century, being swept off one's feet was not enough: one had to reside within the moral compass, and that required education. So Longinus writes:

> Grandeur is particularly dangerous when left on its own, unaccompanied by knowledge, unsteadied, unballasted, abandoned to mere impulse and ignorant temerity. It often needs the curb as well as the spur.[7]

And later:

> I should myself have no hesitation in saying that there is nothing so productive of grandeur as noble emotion in the right place. It inspires and possesses our words with a kind of madness and divine spirit.[8]

To the modern ear there seems to be a paradox here: madness and nobility, we imagine, might well be at loggerheads. But to the Romantics and to Kant in particular there was a unity between a moral framework and the very ability to reach those echelons of the sublime. It is uncertain whether Kant actually read Longinus; what is known, however, was that he was a keen admirer of Burke, to whom I shall now turn.

Burke

Edmund Burke published *A Philosophical Enquiry into the Origin of our Ideas of the Sublime and Beautiful* in 1757. For a man of letters, it was a fashionable subject. The cultured elite had gobbled up Longinus and wanted more; and how he decided to make his mark was to draw a distinct line between what was sublime and what was beautiful. He writes in his preface to the first edition:

> Even Longinus, in his incomparable discourse upon a part of this subject, has comprehended things extremely repugnant to each other, under one common name of 'the sublime'. The abuse of the word 'Beauty' has been still more general, and attended with still worse consequences.[9]

But in his preface to the second edition he makes an important concession to his critics: as long as there is an internal consistency under the headings 'Sublime' and 'Beauty', he declares:

> I am in little pain whether any body chuses to follow the name I give them or not, provided he allows that what I dispose under different heads are in reality different things in nature.[10]

The word 'reality' is what is interesting here: a mere working definition of 'sublimity' is not enough. Burke is referring to an inner state that he wants us to recognize as being in some sense 'true' and, indeed, had 'sublimity' not been *de rigueur* at the time the word might have been a different one. Burke's ambitions are not literary but scientific. In his second preface, he writes:

The use of such enquiries may be very considerable. Whatever turns the soul inward on itself, tends to concenter its forces, and to fit it for greater and stronger flights of science.[11]

Burke is attempting, no less, to construct a scientific theory of the passions, and having set out in his first edition to prove that the strongest passion was the experience of the sublime, by his second his theory is both humbler yet more profound. The experience I am referring to *exists*, he says. Call it what you will.

Burke seems to be seeking out a state of mind in which we are not self-conscious. Usually we act and are aware of acting at the same time, but a sense of the sublime takes over our minds entirely:

The passion caused by the great and sublime in nature, when those causes operate most powerfully, is Astonishment; and astonishment is that state of the soul, in which all its motions are suspended, with some degree of horror. In this case the mind is so entirely filled with its object, that it cannot entertain any other, nor by consequence reason on that object which employs it. Hence arises the great power of the sublime, that far from being produced by them, it anticipates our reasonings, and hurries us on by an irresistible force. Astonishment, as I have said, is the effect of the sublime in its highest degree; the inferior effects are admiration, reverence and respect.[12]

If Burke is right, if horror gives rise to the sublime, logic demands that so will *all* extreme emotion, *all* emotion which is strong enough to appropriate the mind *in toto*. Mere reverence is not powerful enough for Burke; awe is too slight. What he's looking for (and here he's surely mistaken) is abject terror:

> No passion so effectually robs the mind of all its powers of acting and reasoning as fear. For fear being an apprehension of pain or death, it operates in a manner which resembles actual pain. Whatever therefore is terrible, with regard to sight, is sublime too, whether this cause of terror be endued with greatness of dimensions or not; for it is impossible to look on anything as trifling, or contemptible, that may be dangerous.[13]

In other words, if you are in fear for your life, there is no room for irony or politeness, or of thinking one thing and saying another. Of course this is true, yet there might well be a class of 'moods' or 'attitudes' in which self-consciousness disappears, but this in no way means that members of the class are identical or even similar (except in the sense of being absorbing).

Burke makes a second point about the sublime that is surely more persuasive. He invokes 'obscurity' as a necessary condition of it. He writes:

> If I made a drawing of a palace, or a temple, or a landscape, I present a very clear idea of those objects; but then

(allowing for the effect of imitation which is something) my picture can at most affect only as the palace, temple, or landscape would have affected in the reality.[14]

Roger Scruton makes the same point in his paper 'Photography and Representation', namely that a photograph does not *add* anything to its subject, and affects us in much the same way as its subject does: 'The ideal photograph ... stands in a causal relation to its subject and "represents" its subject by reproducing its appearance.'[15] Scruton goes on to suggest that *art* does something more than this, there is *more to understand* in art and *more to know*, which is why, ultimately, art is more exhilarating. Burke anticipates Scruton when he writes:

In reality a great clearness helps but little towards affecting the passions, as it is in some sort an enemy to all enthusiasms whatsoever. ... And I think there are reasons in nature why the obscure idea, when properly conveyed, should be more affecting than the clear. It is our ignorance of things that causes all our admiration, and chiefly excites our passions.[16]

Burke's logic is no better in this instance than where he equates the sublime with 'terror', but he makes an observation that is more convincing. Here, both the sublime and obscurity belong to the class of 'what excites our passions'; again he identifies them as being 'like each other in this respect' yet the overlap, I would argue, is significantly more pronounced. Both art and religion invoke a sense of *mystery*, of *unknowing*, or perhaps it would be more accurate to say, *a different kind of knowing*. The obscure invites questions, invites us to approach and understand. It does not say, 'this is the case', 'this is certain', but throws up a space where getting to know becomes possible.

Burke's third attribute of the sublime is that it should invoke a sense of the infinite. He anticipates Kant when he writes:

> But let it be considered that hardly any thing can strike the mind with its greatness, which does not make some sort of approach towards infinity: which nothing can do whilst we are able to perceive its bounds; but to see an object distinctly, and to perceive its bounds, is one and the same thing.[17]

In Burke's section on 'infinity' he brings together for the first time his three attributes of the sublime:

> Another source of the sublime is infinity; if it does not rather belong to the last. Infinity has a tendency to fill the mind with that sort of delightful horror, which is the most genuine effect, and truest test of the sublime. There are scarce any things which can become the objects of our senses that are really, and in their own nature infinite. But the eye not being able to perceive the bounds of many

things, they seem to be infinite, and they produce the same effects as if they really were so.[18]

Here is Burke at his most philosophical, and Kant will take up the mantle and explore in far more depth how a sense of the infinite affects both the mathematically sublime and the role of the imagination. Meanwhile Burke happily puts his theory to one side and enjoys furnishing us with examples of what he means. Any concept of 'terror' suddenly evaporates. Instead he suggests that the season of spring and young animals are pleasing because 'the imagination is entertained with the promise of something more.'

Frolicking lambs are now considered a source of the sublime, as is Stonehenge (on account of how difficult it must have been to construct) and the starry heaven, because of its 'magnificence' and the fact that it never fails to excite an idea of grandeur. Many of Burke's chapter headings (Light in Building; Colour Considered as Productive of the Sublime; Sound and Loudness; Suddenness; even The Cries of Animals) now become ready sources of the sublime, and the more he adds to the list, the more his 'philosophical enquiry' runs dry, and he becomes like an eager child making lists of exciting things.

Burke should be remembered for his philosophically acute observations, and not for his descent into a more vacuous, modern use of the word 'sublime'.

Kant

Kant wrote about the sublime over a period of some thirty years. The Kant scholar Paul Guyer is dismissive of any so called 'theory', writing that at best it might be of historical interest; and certainly Kant is not sure how much of a role to give to the sublime in his critical philosophy. I will argue that he might have given it significantly more: that its characteristics – or rather, the way the mind is affected by the sublime – is epistemologically the very key he's been searching for, in that if he had been brave enough to develop it, rather than being anxious that it was too dependent on mere imagination, it might have served as the very bridge he was looking for between the theoretical 'understanding' of his first Critique and the 'practical reason' of his second, where morality is given *a priori* status.

In his third Critique he tries to establish the importance of 'judgement', in this case 'aesthetic' judgement. He attempts to solve his famous 'antinomy' – how can something which is merely subjective have objective value? – but although it is agreed he fails to do so, my answer in this essay will be that he does not pose the question correctly, for his description of reality is too prosaic. 'Right' or 'Wrong' is not an appropriate reaction to a reality that is open-ended and *on another ontological level*. However, Kant offers valuable insights, and it is to these I now turn.

Observations on the Beautiful and the Sublime (1764)

Right from the beginning, Kant suggests that the sublime is not reducible to *something out there*, such as a thundering sky or a majestic mountain; rather what interests him is man, and it is the feeling within him that can be termed 'sublime'. In this way he differed from his contemporaries, who took it for granted that beauty was as real as, say, colour. In this first book, Kant makes clear that he is writing as an observer and not as a philosopher. He makes lists, rather than analyses, and it is obvious that he is interested in the ongoing debate that seeks to distinguish 'beauty' from 'the sublime'. We see that it is man's nature that is his first interest. He lists the various emotions that he considers either beautiful or sublime, attributing them to the sexes or nationalities (men have a greater stock of the sublime virtues; women of beautiful ones!). A typical passage begins his second chapter:

> Understanding is sublime, wit is beautiful. Courage is sublime and great, artfulness is little but beautiful … Unselfish zeal to serve is noble; refinement and courtesy are beautiful. Sublime attributes stimulate esteem, but beautiful ones, love … There is many a person whom one esteems much too highly to be able to love him.[19]

A few pages later, his sails now billowing in the wind, it is obvious that the 'sublime attributes' are going to win hands down:

Accordingly, true virtue can be grafted only upon principles such that the more general they are, the more sublime and noble it becomes. These principles are not speculative rules, but the consciousness of a feeling that lives in every human breast and extends itself much further than over the particular grounds of compassion and complaisance. I believe that I sum it all up when I say that it is the feeling of the beauty and the dignity of human nature.[20]

In the Critiques he goes beyond even this definition, but the language is so often dry and abstract, and so determined to fall back on reason to give his thesis status as an *a priori* truth, that Kant's passionate commitment to the sublime often fails to come across.

Critique of Practical Reason (1788)

Kant considers the 'moral law' to be an *a priori* truth. On the back of it, he even builds a case for God. His argument runs that we are not mechanisms of nature because we have free will; and we are free to obey the moral law with our 'supersensible' selves. In other words, man's ability to override his merely sensuous impulses sets him apart from nature. Crowther writes:

In *The Critique of Practical Reason* Kant goes so far as to define 'personality' exclusively in terms of such sublime moral consciousness. On the one hand, it is 'freedom and independence from the mechanism of nature', and on the other hand, the capacity for being 'subject to special laws (pure practical laws given by its own reason).'[21]

Kant calls the relationship between a man's 'moral consciousness' and these 'special laws' respect. But it is interesting that it is man's own powers of reason that are making these laws: his sense of morality and 'moral laws' might be in tune with each other, but ultimately they both sit on one side of the fence: this world. There is no recognition of 'something else beyond'. Nonetheless, Kant wants a hierarchy: reason has precedence over mere feeling, and can establish an *a priori* truth. 'Respect' is the link between subjective feeling and that truth. (This runs parallel, it seems to me, to the disinterestedness necessary to reach an aesthetic truth: feeling, interest, sympathy cannot be part of the *a priori* universe.) He writes:

> Respect ... is not a feeling received through outside influence, rather one self-produced by a rational concept and therefore specifically distinct from feelings of the first kind.'[22]

Crowther sums up Kant's position very succinctly:

> It is important to note that, here, Kant's conception of moral feeling is the reverse of the position set out in the Observations. Moral consciousness does not start from some affectionate feeling for humankind which is then generalized into a universal principle; we find instead that

moral feeling (i.e. respect) is the outcome of our recognition that the will is necessarily subject to the moral law. It arises, in other words, from our self-transcendence to the universal.[23]

The 'sublime' moral consciousness, therefore, is a vehicle that might take us to God.

Critique of Judgement 1791

Kant sets out his ambitions for his third Critique in his introduction; he explains that 'there is still in the family of our higher cognitive faculties a middle term between understanding and reason.'[24] This turns out to be judgement, which in turn is either 'determinant' (when it can subsume a particular under a universal) or 'reflective', 'when the particular is given and the universal has to be found for it.'[25] He then goes on to say that he's already taken care of 'determinant' judgement in his first Critique. What is going to interest him is 'reflective' judgement.

By its very nature, then, certainty is something Kant is going to have to forsake, and in this Critique he is going to assign an important role to the imagination. Clayton Crockett in his book *A Theology of the Sublime,* is particularly interesting on this subject. He points to a long-standing tussle between Kant's determination to have reason as master, and his understanding that imagination has to be in equal partnership with it.

Crockett sees this third Critique as having bearing on his first, and draws our attention to the fact that Kant alters the status he gives to the imagination in the two editions of that Critique. In the first, Kant writes that 'there are two stems of human knowledge, namely, sensibility and understanding, which perhaps spring forth from a common, but to us unknown, root.' (A15/B29). Crockett writes:

> Heidegger suggests that the transcendental power of imagination is the root of both stems. In the second edition of the *Critique of Pure Reason*, the independent faculty of imagination with all of its productive power of synthesis is collapsed into the faculty of understanding. Heidegger claims that 'Kant did not carry through with the more original interpretation from the transcendental power of imagination ... On the contrary: Kant shrank back from his unknown root.' ... Kant fears the power of imagination because it threatens the objectivity he has fought so hard to establish, at the cost of limiting our knowledge to things as they appear to us.[26]

It is not surprising, therefore, that Kant (and his commentators) also waver in the status they give the sublime. Kant's mood seems to shift as he wrote his third Critique, and commentators are apt to take what they want and bracket what they don't. It seems that *psychologically* Kant wants to give a central role to the limitlessness of the imagination and its ability to apprehend the infinite; but *philosophically* wants to give the central role to reason. First, then, I shall consider Kant as the philosopher, trying to schematize and build the great edifice of his metaphysics with a steady hand.

First of all he distinguishes between the beautiful and the sublime. They are both 'pleasing'; neither are exclusively empirically based nor based on reason, but rather 'reflection' and 'an indeterminate reference to concepts.' They both profess to be 'universally valid in respect of every subject', though the claims are directed to pleasure and not to knowledge of the object. But after these few similarities the sublime is defined by what the beautiful is not:

> There are, however, also important and striking differences between the two. The beautiful in nature is a question of the form of the object, and this consists in limitation, whereas the sublime is to be found in an object even devoid of form, so far as it immediately involves, or else by its presence provokes, a representation of limitlessness, yet with a super-added thought of its totality.[27]

There is food here both for those who prefer a theory of the sublime to be essentially an *aesthetic* theory (i.e. applicable to art), in which case the possibility of form is necessary, and those, like myself, who see the potential of Kant's theory as a core constituent of a theory of knowledge. The word 'even' as in 'even devoid of form' allows a window for 'form', as does the last phrase, where we have a 'thought' of its totality. Burke would happily resist either admission; for him the sublime is characterized by a departure of self, there is certainly no 'thought' able to be entertained. But Kant has at this stage not made clear the dialectic between other and self that he sees as the core of the experience.

When Kant then distinguishes between our responses to the sublime and the beautiful, describing the beautiful as 'compatible with charms and a playful imagination', whereas the feeling of the sublime is an emotion 'that seems to be no sport, but dead earnest in the affairs of the imagination' (thereby calling it a 'negative pleasure'),[28] he plays into the hands of the aestheticians, but then he becomes more interesting. He says that natural beauty is 'preadapted to our power of judgement',[29] in other words is familiar and comfortable to us, while the sublime performs an 'outrage on the imagination'[30]. However, he then makes a very important caveat:

The sublime, in the strict sense of the word, cannot be contained in any sensuous form, but rather concerns ideas of reason, which, although no adequate presentation of them is possible, may be excited and called into the mind by that very inadequacy itself which does not admit of sensuous presentation. Thus the broad ocean agitated by storms cannot be called sublime. Its aspect is horrible, and one must have stored one's mind in advance with a rich stock of ideas, if such an intuition is to raise it to the pitch of a feeling which is itself sublime – sublime because the mind had been incited to abandon sensibility and employ itself upon ideas involving higher finality.[31]

This is the first time that Kant makes the point that the sublime is something about *us* and not something just 'out there'. It is also the first time that we hear about a conflict within us: that between imagination and reason, incommensurable faculties from which the French post-modern philosopher Lyotard derives his famous 'differend':

> This differend is to be found at the heart of sublime feeling: at the encounter of the two 'absolutes' equally 'present' to thought, the absolute whole when it conceives, the absolutely measured when it presents. 'Meeting' conveys very little, it is more of a confrontation, for, in accordance with its destination, which is to be whole, the absolute concepts demand to be presented.[32]

Lyotard takes the sublime where it needs to go, and is happy to attempt to resolve the differend through a 'dialectic'. He admits that this is an Hegelian rather than Kantian notion, but I think he is right. Kant systematically (and desperately) tries to contain all on the same level; he works out his conflict by giving it a temporal structure. To begin with, we have to be cultured beings, 'rich in a stock of ideas' – uneducated peasants are incapable of having a sense of the sublime; then, we let our imagination play havoc, and finally, reason reigns us in again and is victor. But Lyotard is much more adventurous:

It is precisely, says reason to the imagination, in showing that you cannot 'comprehend' more magnitudes in a single intuition than you are doing that would show you can, for in order to show the limit, you must also show beyond the limit. Such that the pleasure in infinitude, which is mine, is already latent in the unhappiness you feel in your finitude. The process consists in displacing the examination of judgment from its (negative) quality to its (assertive) modality. You say that … is not, but you affirm it.[33]

In Kant's description of the mathematically sublime, Lyotard's hope for a dialectic to resolve the differend seems to me to not only be reasonable but one of which Kant himself might approve. After having explained that '"sublime" is the name given to what is absolutely great', he expands:

Its mere greatness, regarded even as devoid of form, is able to convey a universally communicable delight … not … in the Object, for the latter may be formless, but … a delight in an extension affecting the imagination itself.[34]

In other words, the delight is self-reflexive, it is caused by an event that happens in one's own imagination. This event Kant makes very clear. Reason by its nature needs to grasp the totality of a thing, but when it cannot (as is the case with the Pyramids or St Peter's in Rome), 'the imagination recoils upon itself, but in so doing succumbs to an emotional delight.'[35] Kant writes:

But precisely because there is a striving in our imagination towards progress ad infinitum, while reason demands absolute totality, as a real idea, that same inability on the part of our faculty for the estimation of the magnitude of things of the world of sense to attain to this idea, is the awakening of a feeling of a supersensible faculty within us … The sublime is that, the mere capacity of thinking which evidences a faculty of mind transcending every standard of sense.[36]

This definition chimes closely with Kant's assessment of the sublime in his *Critique of Practical Reason.* 'Moral consciousness' is also 'supersensible' because it obeys a moral law over and above one's self-interest: that is the very thing that makes it 'sublime'. Here is another case of transcendence over 'the things of the world' and 'every standard of sense', because the imagination cannot cope on its own, and we have to transcend our 'inability'. This emotional openness to what we do not know strikes at the very core, I believe, of an account of the sublime. Reason demands 'absolute totality' but as Kant concedes, it does not get it. He writes:

But the point of capital importance is that the mere ability even to think it as a whole indicates a faculty of mind transcending every standard of sense. … the mere ability even to think the given infinite without contradiction, is something that requires the presence in the human mind of a faculty that is itself supersensible.[37]

So now we have the 'given infinite' and the 'supersensible' faculty of the human mind, and indeed, he momentarily forgets his insistence that objects of nature are not sublime (just the feeling within) when he says, 'Nature, therefore, is sublime in such of its phenomena as in their intuition convey the idea of their infinity.'[38] Moments later, however, Kant is reminding us all over again that it is not nature, but rather:

the cast of mind in appreciating it that we have to estimate as sublime ... Who would apply the term 'sublime' even to shapeless mountain masses towering one above the other in wild disorder with their pyramids of ice, or to the dark tempestuous ocean, or such like things? But in the contemplation of them, without any regard to their form, the mind abandons itself to the imagination and to a reason placed, though quite apart from any definite end, in conjunction therewith, and merely broadening its view, and it feels itself elevated in its own estimate of itself on finding all the might of imagination still unequal to its ideas.[39]

It is evident in this passage that Kant isn't so much interested in a dialectic, a confrontation: he wants an outright winner, reason, because ultimately he still has his eye on the objectivity of knowledge. He wants to say: the sublime might first overwhelm us, but having been overwhelmed we are brought to a new surmise of ourselves: as rational, moral creatures, in some sense superior to what at first seemed superior to us:

Therefore the feeling of the sublime in nature is respect for
our own vocation, which we attribute to an Object of
nature by a certain subreption (substitution of a respect for
the Object of nature in place of one for the idea of
humanity in our own self – the Subject) and this renders, as
it were, intuitable the supremacy of our cognitive faculties
on the rational side over the greatest faculty of sensibility.[40]

So actually, all that wonder about nature, says Kant, is a red
herring; our astonishment should really be directed at
ourselves. That great thundering sky is nothing compared with
our ability to stand back from it: and therein lies our delight, in
this enhanced consciousness of our cognitive faculties:

Bold, overhanging, and, as it were, threatening rocks,
thunderclouds piled up the vault of heaven, borne along
with flashes and peals, volcanoes in all their violence of
destruction, hurricanes leaving desolation in their track, the
boundless ocean rising with rebellious force, the high
waterfall of some mighty river, and the like, make our
power of resistance of trifling moment in comparison with
their might. But once our own position is secure, their
aspect is all the more attractive for its fearfulness and we
readily call these objects sublime, because they raise the
forces of the soul above the height of vulgar commonplace,
and discover within us a power of resistance of quite
another kind, which gives us courage to be able to measure
ourselves against the seeming omnipotence of nature.[41]

Here suddenly we find Burke's influence, and indeed descriptions that found themselves in art and romantic poetry for the next hundred years – until the images which had initially excited people themselves became cliché and could no longer do their magic. Kant here gives the prize to human beings, whose 'souls have been raised above the height of the vulgar commonplace', but the soul can't be taken from the *radically other*, the two are momentarily inter-dependent. What we cannot fathom, count, compute or make sense of is suddenly the *cause* of our self-knowledge. Kant says that in the same way as we are not aware of our bodies unless they are undergoing pain or experiencing pleasure, we are not aware of our souls unless we are able to 'measure ourselves against the seeming omnipotence of nature.' In other words, the sublime is now beginning to have an epistemological dimension over and above an aesthetic one.

If Kant's account of the mathematically sublime sees him at his most systematic (and commentators are right to draw attention to the fact the Pyramids are only thought to be 'sublime' if seen at an optimum distance, neither too close nor too far), the remainder of his Analytic occasionally sees Kant approach mystical status. Authentic self-consciousness becomes the route to the transcendental. Kant writes:

Everything that provokes this feeling in us, including the might of nature which challenges our strength, is then, though improperly, called sublime, and it is only under presupposition of this idea within us, and in relation to it, that we are capable of attaining to the idea of the sublimity of that Being which inspires deep respect in us, not by the mere display of its might in nature, but more by the faculty which is planted in us of estimating that might without fear, and of regarding our estate as exalted above it.

So suddenly God has made an entrance, and not just God but the possibility of a relationship with God, which is 'respect'. There are catalysts: call them the infinite, the mighty, the powerful, or as Kant does, merely *nature*, and these draw out ourselves to such an extent that 'we are capable of attaining to the idea of the sublimity of that Being which inspires deep respect in us.' God himself has quite suddenly become 'sublime' and His sublimity reveals to us our own sublimity. *Moral consciousness* was termed *sublime* in his previous critique; now *Being* is, and the relationship between the two is the realisation that we have the faculty 'planted in us of estimating (nature's) might without fear, and of regarding our estate above it.'

This is extraordinary stuff, as he begins to discuss the relationship between a creator and his creation, for he says, the faculty has been 'planted in us.'

Yet later, in Book II of *The Analytic of the Sublime*, having made what seems to be a final assessment on the nature of the sublime, namely that it 'must in every case have reference to our way of thinking, i.e. to maxims directed to giving the intellectual side of our nature and the ideas of reason supremacy over sensibility', he immediately refers back to the role of the imagination:

> For though the imagination, no doubt, finds nothing beyond the sensible world to which it can lay hold, still this thrusting aside of the sensible barriers gives it a feeling of being unbounded; and that removal is thus a presentation of the infinite. As such it can never be anything more than a negative presentation – but still it expands the soul. Perhaps there is no more sublime passage in the Jewish Law than the commandment: Thou shalt not make unto thee any graven image, or any likeness of any thing that is in heaven or on earth, or under the earth *et cetera*.[42]

These three: theology, unboundedness, imagination, are all closely linked for Kant; and no more so that in a footnote later on in the book:

> Perhaps there has never been a more sublime utterance, or a thought more sublimely expressed, than the well known inscription upon the Temple of Isis (Mother Nature): 'I am all that is, and that was, and that ever shall be, and no mortal hath raised the veil from my face.'[43]

Suddenly, where is reason, where is the love of thought? Kant heralded both the Romantics and the formal beginnings of aesthetics with his work. Yet it is quite clear that his heart belongs both to Nature and Mystery. Indeed, this is what he has to say about art:

> If a man with taste enough to judge of works of fine art with the greatest correctness and refinement readily quits the room in which he meets with those beauties that minister to vanity or, at least, social joys, and betakes himself to the beautiful in nature, so that he may there find as it were a feast for his soul in a train of thought which he can never completely evolve, we will then regard this his choice even with veneration, and give him credit for a beautiful soul, to which no connoisseur or art collector can lay claim on the score of the interest which his objects have for him.[44]

Suddenly, then, an interest in fine art has to do with socializing and vanity. Where has some universal value disappeared to, to resolve his antinomy of taste? It is when Kant is off his guard, rather than being at his cleverest, that his true opinions and passions spill out of him. At the end of his second Critique, he declares that his two loves are the stars without him and the moral law within him. His theory of the sublime embraces both, and yet somehow his inconsistencies obscure what is potentially a hugely exciting component of a theory of knowledge.

Conclusion

Burke writes in his introduction to the second edition of his book that we should not hold him to a singular definition of the sublime, but that is not the point. The reality is out there, 'sublime' is but a tag. More than a definition of 'sublime' therefore, what I am seeking is the truth behind the general concept. The sublime is not something simply 'out there'; rather it seems to be a dynamic operation within our own souls, and Longinus, Burke and Kant, I believe, would agree with me. Longinus, though a literary critic rather than a philosopher, is concerned with freshness of feeling, with authenticity. Burke emphasizes the direction of the arrow: what is out there is causing something in here. The sublime can never be a deliberate quest, we have no power over it – in theological terms, we are looking at 'grace'.

It was Kant, however, who made me understand that at its most fundamental a theory of the sublime is part of a larger theory of knowledge. But Kant was anxious that mere 'imagination' could not provide the ballast he was looking for. He is also mistaken, I believe, to express his theory in rigid, temporal terms – first this, then that – the experience talks far more with a clashing of opposites, a dialectic. I want to finish with a paragraph in which, I think, Kant gets it exactly right:

The mind feels itself set in motion in the representation of the sublime in nature, whereas in the aesthetic judgement upon what is beautiful therein it is in restful contemplation.

This movement, especially in its inception, may be compared with a vibration, i.e. with a rapidly alternating repulsion and attraction produced by one and the same Object. The point of excess for the imagination (towards which it is driven in the apprehension of the intuition) is like an abyss in which it fears to lose itself.[45]

Kant is describing the rapid alternation of fear and longing, attraction and repulsion. For Kant, this is no mere, pleasant contemplation of the sublime. The sublime rests precariously on the edge of an abyss, and we do not know what we will find.

Chapter Two

Knowledge and the Sublime

Introduction

In my first chapter I suggested that Kant needs to look to another ontological level in order to solve his 'antinomy of taste'. Here I suggest that the key to such a level lies in an encounter with the sublime. I will also suggest that such an encounter is essentially *epistemological* rather than *aesthetic*. To this end, I will

a) locate the space within which the sublime resides. In particular, I shall quote Robert Frost's poem, *Stopping by Woods on a Snowy Evening*.

b) Introduce Hilary Lawson's book *Closure* and the paradigm I shall use for the explication of my argument. I shall look at Lawson's critique of Kant's theory of knowledge.

c) Consider other current theories of knowledge. In particular, I shall look at the epistemology known as 'critical realism' and compare it with Lawson's own theory of knowledge.

d) Use Lawson's paradigm of openness and closure as a way of locating the sublime; appraise his own account of how art and religion attract us insofar as they are essentially *unknowable*.

e) Finally, assess whether it is more reasonable to locate Kant's theory of the sublime within his epistemology or promote it as a new theory of aesthetics.

The Other Shore: the Sublime in Poetry

Poetry naturally lends itself to a concept of the sublime. In book six of Virgil's *Aeneid*, the dead plead with Charon the ferryman to transport them across the river Styx so they might reach the fields of Elysium. Virgil writes:

> *tendebantque manus ripae ulterioris amore*

> 'And they stretched out their hands, in yearning for the other shore.'[46]

The word Virgil uses for 'yearning' is *amor*, more commonly translated as 'love'. The restless souls have no conception of what lies ahead for them on the other shore, but they *yearn* for this *other place*, and more, they *love what is unknown*. In the year 400 C.E. Augustine could write, 'You have made us for yourself, O Lord, and our heart is restless until it rests in you.' In German the word is *Sehnsucht*, a compound of the word *sehren*, to long for, and *Sucht*, which means anxiety, addiction, obsession. Both Goethe and Schiller have written well-known poems about *Sehnsucht*, and multiple composers including Beethoven, Schubert and Wagner have set the poems to music. I believe such a feeling, however it is translated and whichever word is used, is universal, cross-cultural, and the very essence of what it is to be human.

Another poet who perfectly illustrates this yearning is Robert Frost, in his poem *Stopping by Woods on a Snowy Evening*. The rider is suddenly held by the mystery of the moment, by its 'otherness'. His horse represents the world as he knows it, the familiar:

> Whose woods these are I think I know,
> His house is in the village though;
> He will not see me stopping here
> To watch his woods fill up with snow.
>
> My little horse must think it queer
> To stop without a farmhouse near
> Between the woods and frozen lake
> The darkest evening of the year.
>
> He gives his harness bells a shake
> To ask if there is some mistake.
> The only other sound's the sweep
> Of easy wind and downy flake.
>
> The woods are lovely, dark and deep,

> But I have promises to keep
> And miles to go before I sleep,
> And miles to go before I sleep.[47]

The object of the rider's fascination is unclear: both Burke and Kant define the sublime in terms of its 'obscurity' and 'lack of clarity'. There are landmarks noticeable only in their absence: no farmhouse is near, the rider is not 'by' the woods, nor 'by' the lake but 'between' them; it is the darkest evening of the year, yet he yearns to enter the woods which are 'lovely, dark and deep.' They are 'lovely', but of course it is too dark to see them. Again, sublimity lies not in the object itself but the feelings of the observer: Kant reiterates this point, nothing is intrinsically sublime, it is only the event in the soul which can rightly be called so. The rider is lured into those woods, not because they delight him in an easy sense, not because they are 'beautiful', but perversely, because they represent death, a threshold to the other. The horse reminds him to go on, he jangles his harness, and, he remembers, he has 'promises to keep' – he has to remain committed to an earthly life. Nonetheless he remains mesmerized, and the last two lines of the poem are repeated: he is being lured by death, extinction of self, what is other to him. But he has miles to go, and promises to keep. The bliss of sleep must be resisted. For now, at least.

The rider in the poem has a choice, between the closed world which he knows and that which is beyond it, which he does not know and which he craves. This breaking-out of the familiar world into something 'other', which I hold to be the very core of the sublime experience, is epistemologically important. Letting go of old categories to enter a new is the human prerogative. The sublime is an uncharted space. Hilary Lawson's description of such a 'letting go' and its implications for the acquisition of new, authentic, individual understanding is a central tenet of my argument, and it is to him I now turn.

A paradigm: Openness and closure

Longinus' 'authenticity', Kant's 'indeterminacy', Burke's 'astonishment', all affirm the unchartedness of the sublime. But it is Hilary Lawson's book *Closure* (2001) that will provide me with the paradigm I shall be using for this essay. His theory – that human beings need closure but that closure is not the whole truth – is an all-embracing one. By 'closure', Lawson refers first and foremost to language. By naming things, we categorize them and make them knowable. By naming things, we can have a correspondence theory of truth. But such a truth would remain a truth only within an agreed framework – *a posteriori*: like Kant, Lawson wants more from truth, and yet postmodernism has reduced culture to so many alternative descriptions of reality none of which are more 'true' than any other. Lawson sees himself as doing for culture as Gödel did for mathematics, namely by exposing the necessity for an unknowable meta-narrative. He argues that modern descriptions of reality are only that, modern descriptions, using language that is already circumscribed. Self-reflexivity cannot approach truth, but falls back on itself. Lawson describes the problem, when he argues that 'the attempt to provide in language a total symbolic system that describes the relation between language and the world must fail because language and its relationship to the world is not part of the world and therefore cannot be described by it.'[48]

Lawson describes the Western philosophers' 'Great Project' to provide an accurate description of reality as being doomed to failure, and declares that the seed of its own destruction was there from its outset. It is paradoxical for language to say anything ultimate about itself. Wittgenstein throws out his theory of the *Tractatus Logico-philosophicus* with his famous last line, 'What we cannot speak about we must pass over in silence.'[49] Lawson quotes Wittgenstein as perfectly understanding the limits of linguistic philosophy: 'in order to be able to draw a limit to thought, we should have to find both sides of the limit thinkable (i.e. we should have to be able to think what cannot be thought)'.[50]

Lawson, I believe, is ground-breaking in his escape route from the circularity of language. He argues for the 'adoption of an alternative notion of the world. A notion in which the world is not held as a thing or a combination of things. For the moment such an outlook will be indentified as the holding of the world as not-thing.'[51] And he is surely right: the world as not-thing is ontologically prior to the world as a combination of things, as dictated by language. Lawson recognizes an ally in

Kant: men categorize in order to control and understand, but ultimate truth necessarily eludes them. Lawson writes:

> From forest to tree, from beech to oak, from branch to leaf, we have things it would appear for every part and aspect of the world. Although we may not choose to do so, there is in principle no corner left untouched, no crevice unfilled, no location in which some thing cannot be found. In proposing that the world is held as not-thing, these distinctions are to be seen not as the outcome of distinctions in the world but as the outcome of language, it is not simply that we could have named these things differently, or have made different distinctions, but that the possibility of dividing the world into things at all is itself the outcome of a process of which language is a part. The world is not either divided into things or the result of the combination of things, nor is itself a thing.[52]

Not only are Kant's arguments surprisingly similar, but even his motives are: both Lawson and Kant want *a priori* truth and are happy to sacrifice *a posteriori* 'knowledge' at its altar. But Lawson is suspicious of Kant's use of *noumena* to rescue his metaphysics. He acknowledges that he needs them, but suggests that their function is too specific and therefore remain a part of the world rather than truly separate from it. In my own terminology (see chapter three), there is not a sufficient *rupture* from the familiar. He argues:

Kant's world of appearances, his description of experience and knowledge, cannot contain that which causes experience or that which has the experience. Reality and the self in this sense are therefore for Kant beyond the world of appearance and thus transcendent. Kant identifies these elements that lie outside of experience as noumena. In this description and with it the postulation of a noumenal world can be seen an attempt to name the unnameable. For 'the noumenal world' seeks to identify something beyond closure, something which cannot be identified, for it cannot be experienced or known.[53]

Lawson explains that Kant talks about 'the noumenal world' when he might as well have talked about 'reality' or 'the self', but that he does not use these terms 'because they would at once be part of our knowledge and thus part of the world of appearance … He therefore seeks to point outwards from his system of closure to a world that cannot be identified as any particular thing but which is necessarily other.'[54] However, Lawson considers that his attempt has failed precisely because 'this world is offered as the site of the transcendental object and the transcendental subject, in which case we already have an understanding of that which is supposedly beyond understanding.' Lawson continues:

As soon as we imagine the noumenal world as the underlying reality that lies behind the artifice of experience generated by the combination of intuition and concept, we have introduced into the 'noumenal world' an element of closure ... Although therefore Kant presents the noumenal world as an empty notion, it has necessarily an exoteric element.[55]

And Lawson then gives Kant the solution to the problem: 'In order to understand Kant's notion of the noumenal world we must therefore not understand it, and it is in this sense, esoteric.'[56] In other words, Lawson might look at mystical theology not as some wishy-washy, romantic notion about something other and higher *et cetera*, but necessary as a fundamental building block of knowledge.

Lawson has identified the core of my argument: *In order to understand we must not understand; in order to know we must not know.* This is the place, I believe, Kant might have sought with his theory of the sublime: paradoxically, this is the epistemological ballast he was looking for. Yet the abyss that he peered into was ultimately to repel rather than attract him, and 'reason' was to get the upper hand.

Theories of Knowledge

Central to philosophers' hopes is that humans are able to know what is true. If humans are unable to *know* something then there is nothing that can be *known*, hence no truth. So what are the conditions necessary for man to be said to *know* something? And is there more than one kind of truth? If there is such a thing as knowledge of the sublime, how would it be different from the knowledge of a linguistic proposition?

The correspondence theory of truth holds that for a proposition to be true, it needs to correspond to facts in the world. So, the proposition, 'The cat is on the mat' is true only when there is a real cat and a real mat, and the cat is indeed, on it.

The problem with this theory is that it depends on experience. If I have never seen a cat before, how would I *know* that this was a cat that I was looking at? I believe it is a cat, because I have seen pictures in books that tell me it is a cat. But how do I *know* the books I have read are telling me the truth? There is no *criterion* to decide whether a particular belief I have is true or not, if I do not have first-hand experience of it.

There is also a problem about the nature of universals. When we use the word 'cat', what exactly are we thinking of? Do we count a lion as a cat, for example? What is the essence of catness by which a cat can be counted as a cat? Do we define objects by how they appear or their function? When is a bed a sofa? When is a sofa a bed? Again, there is no absolute criterion. At first a correspondence theory seems like common sense, and the fact that there is some actual *correspondence* (whatever that might mean) between language and reality seems hopeful; but what exactly is the nature of that correspondence? Vincent Brummer clarifies the problem well:

In order to achieve the necessary equivalent between propositions and facts (without which they cannot be similar) the theory has to define the structure of the facts in terms of the structure of propositions. The result is an ontology derived from grammar.[57]

But if a chasm remains between language and its referents, and 'truth' remains elusive, the alternatives are equally unsatisfactory. A 'coherence' theory of truth rejects the world entirely in favour of propositions that are made up of prior propositions that are known to be true, in the same way as a batch of yoghurt is used to make more yoghurt. Nothing completely new, therefore, can ever be discovered or said; everything is inter-textual. Propositions might be considered 'true', but only in a trite and ultimately meaningless way. Man would know only what he knows; truth is made by man and man alone. And even that statement cannot be considered true: it is just a further sentence within a language game. Deconstructionists would support such a theory, adding that 'truth' is a cover-up for ideology and power.

Rejecting these theories, pragmatists have veered ever further from some concept of 'absolute truth'. Some philosophers have been content with 'something to live by.' C.S. Peirce wanted objective truth, but stumbled on where to find it, in the end suggesting that it is 'what the scientific community agree upon.'[58] That is quite a tall order to begin with: are scientific models not eternally modified by some new understanding? Is truth not available to individuals, only to communities? William James wanted to promote Christianity by arguing that Christians lived happier and more moral lives than those who were not Christians. But does that really hold water as an argument in search of some kind of 'truth'?

Reductionists, such as A.J. Ayer and the logical positivists, asserted the need to verify a proposition before it could count as 'true'.[59] Propositions which could not be verified, e.g. which contained abstract notions of goodness and beauty, were simply discounted as meaningless. But if you try to pin-point truth it will escape you, in the same way as the present moment cannot escape belonging to the past. Just because you cannot verify the truth does not mean that the truth does not exist. If a blind man were to go into a room which was painted either red, white or blue, and made three different assertions as to its colour, the fact that he does not know which of those three assertions is the true one, let alone be able to verify that statement, does not mean that one of those three statements has not 'hit upon' the truth. Just because knowledge is impossible, does not mean that truth is also a chimera. The reason why human beings operate so successfully is that they instinctively hit upon the truth so often, *without* being able to pin it down.

Logicians try to hold truth down, but it won't be held, because only deductive statements can be held, and prior assertions about the world will necessarily be hit and miss. However, that does not mean objective truth does not exist.

What is, is: the first rule of ontology. Things *did* happen in a particular way, we just don't know which way. But why are some (indeed most) philosophers so adamant that you have to know that you know something before it can really *count* as knowledge? Isn't it possible to *know* something without realizing it? Such is the claim of the critical realists, and it is to them I now turn.

Critical Realism

The theologian Anthony Monti uses the epistemology of critical realism as a means of justifying truth claims in both art and religion. In his paper 'Types and Symbols of Eternity' Monti writes:

Previously, natural theology was thought to consist of deductive 'proofs' (in which form they have been demolished by philosophers, scientists and theologians respectively). Now this search is thought to operate by means of what Michael Polanyi calls tacit understanding – in which we know 'more than we can tell', through intuitive acts of apprehension that go beyond strictly logical inference. If this is the case, then works of art, which themselves work by intuitive acts of apprehension, could in fact *be* what so many people experience them as being – namely, vehicles for the presence of God.[60]

If Lawson is critical of Kant's *noumena* for reasons of having 'too much content', how much more critical would he be of Monti's hopes to find 'the presence of God' in what is other. (The 'metaphysics of presence' will be given a hard time by both the mystics and post-modernists in Chapter Three.) Nonetheless, critical realism has a lot in common with both Kant and Lawson, in raising the truth status of 'intuitive acts of apprehension.' What is also appealing is that the model is taken from the natural sciences and advocated by the atheist Michael Polanyi in his book *Personal Knowledge* (1958). Monti quotes the Anglican scholar, N.T. Wright as giving the most succinct definition of critical realism:

> This is a way of describing the process of 'knowing' that acknowledges the *reality of the thing known as something other than the knower* (hence 'realism') while also fully acknowledging that the only access we have to this reality lies along the spiralling path of appropriate dialogue or conversation between the knower and the thing known (hence 'critical').[61]

What Monti is pleased with is the fact that critical realism acknowledges, in a post-Kantian way, that our ways of cognition are culturally conditioned. Monti's hope is that he can somehow restore the self-perception of the humanities; he wants them to consider themselves 'truth-seeking' rather than unconditionally relative. He likes the word (and I do too) 'dialogue', suggesting that despite the absence of an indisputable foundation of knowledge, there *is* truth to be found in 'the provisionality of some initial point of view,' and he quotes Polanyi to support him, who suggests that the purpose of science is 'to achieve a frame of mind in which I may hold firmly to what I believe to be true, even though I know it might conceivably be false.'[62]

Post-modernism exposes the circularity of knowledge, reducing, therefore, any knowledge to no knowledge; but critical realism embraces the 'hermeneutic circle'. Polanyi observes, 'Any enquiry into our ultimate beliefs can be consistent only if it presupposes its own conclusions. It must be intentionally circular.'[63]

Monti suggests that circularity works as a theory of genuine knowledge when there is a 'dialogue' contained within it, a story and a counter-story:

Between direct confirmation and direct confrontation, events or objects may modify or subvert my existing story…some stories or hypotheses are better or more adequate than others, which in turn suggests (though again it does not prove) that those better, more adequate stories are so because they have somehow got more of a hold upon something real, out there, to which they are responding.[64]

Monti suggests this is the 'realism' part of critical realism: in science, theories work because they bear some relation to the way things are, which is different from saying that any isolated hypothesis is verifiable. He suggests Polanyi's concept of 'tacit understanding', whereby 'We know more than we can tell', calls upon intuition as a way of eliciting the truth. He quotes Polkinghorne's definition of tacit understanding as that 'which cannot be given exhaustive prior characterization but which has to be perceived intuitively.'[65]

Monti implicitly asks the question in his book, *A Natural Theology of the Arts*, 'what do we know without knowing that we know it?' and uses critical realism to make a case for the existence of God. God is presupposed as a *subsidiary awareness* in the same way, according to Polanyi's theory, as we have a subsidiary awareness of a lot of information (e.g. the hammer's weight, balance *et cetera*) as we strike in a nail. There is a *focal awareness* that is on the nail, but the hammer becomes, as it were, a part of ourselves (Polanyi suggests we *indwell* in the hammer.)

An intuitive knowledge of God, in the way we use language as well as in the way we respond to the arts, is the epistemological equivalent to Polanyi's account of subsidiary awareness. Regarding language, Monti regards it as a 'semantic marker' to the transcendent. If Derrida argues that 'the age of the sign' is now over, because we can no longer presume that language has God as its guarantor, Monti sides with George Steiner, and quotes from his book *Real Presences*:

Deconstruction teaches us that where there is no "face of God" for the semantic marker to turn to, there can be no transcendent or decidable intelligibility. The break with the postulate of the sacred is the break with any stable, potentially ascertainable meaning of meaning.[66]

Monti recognizes in Steiner's words an account of 'our experience of "the real presence" of an Other beyond ourselves in the poem, the painting or the symphony'. He quotes from Steiner again:

So far as it wagers on meaning, an account of the act of reading, in the fullest sense, of the act of the reception and internalization of significant forms within us, is a metaphysical and, in the last analysis, a theological one. The ascription of beauty to truth and to meaning is either a rhetorical flourish, or it is a piece of theology. It is a theology, explicit or suppressed, masked or avowed, substantive or imaged, which underwrites the presumption of creativity, or significance in our encounters with text, with music, with art. The meaning of meaning is a transcendent postulate.[67]

Monti's book is both a bold and passionately argued account of what might constitute this sense of the other. The title of his second chapter 'The metaphysic of flexible openness' resonates with Lawson's own account of openness. However, as we have seen, Lawson resists giving the other any kind of content. Monti, conversely, quotes Gunton's ideas about the nature of 'spirit' which is 'to do with the crossing of boundaries … That which is or has spirit is able to be open to that which is other than itself, to move into relation with the other.'[68] And, ultimately, Monti is going to want to give even more flesh to his concept of 'other': by his final chapter, not only is 'God' located within 'subsidiary awareness,' but all three persons of the Christian Trinity. It is not within the remit of this essay to argue with him; rather, I wish to suggest that the fleshing out of what is other is not *necessary* for a meaningful encounter with what is other.

Lawson's Epistemology: Openness and Closure in Art and Religion

As a preface to his chapter on 'The structure of knowledge', Lawson writes:

> Knowledge is hierarchical and subdivided, unlimited and pyramidal. Its closures are interdependent, and have the appearance of being largely complete; and the future structure and use of the closures of cultural space is unpredictable. Each of these characteristics flows from the character of closure.[69]

Contained within these few words is a summary of how Lawson believes knowledge happens. But what is exciting about Lawson's epistemology, is the fact that he believes that new knowledge happens at the level of the *individual*. We are a far cry from Peirce's assertion that knowledge is founded on 'what the scientific community agrees upon'. Although Lawson agrees with the postmodernists that individuals 'realise their individual space in the context of the marks of language and the current organisation of those marks prevalent in the culture,'[70] Lawson is going to show that 'the structure of knowledge reflects the character of the search for closure on the part of individuals. This is because the closures of cultural space are the product of a history of individual realisations of closure.'[71] Lawson goes on to show how individuals *think* that they have achieved closure by, for example, the naming of geographical locations, but how on close examination, e.g. 'the Matterhorn', 'New York', 'the Thames' – how would one be able to argue where the mountain, city, river, begins and ends? And is there more than mere geography involved when it comes to the tagging process? At what point does the Thames become a part of the sea?

Knowledge, argues Lawson, at the level of society, looks to 'those sets of marks of cultural space that carry "authority"' and the authority is realised 'by those individuals within the culture who are deemed competent in a relevant sphere'[72] but that authority is given to them *by the individual*. 'Closures can only be realised by individuals and not groups or cultures' and the closures realised by each individual will be slightly different from each other. In other words, Lawson is showing us how a break from the 'hermeneutic circularity of knowledge' is possible. It is possible to modify and even disagree with the knowledge that is being offered. It is possible to remain *open to something else.*

Lawson takes his terms, 'openness' and 'closure' and uses them to describe other forms of knowledge. By exposing the impossibility of absolute closure on even the most prosaic aspects of knowledge, we are ready to submit our experience of art and religion to more openness. Lawson writes, 'Religion as a system of belief, backed by an institution, provides an explanation and a description of the world, and in this respect functions as a closure or linked set of closures.'[73] Yet, conversely, religion is concerned with a 'search for openness. What impels the religious attitude is not only the provision of a system of belief and thus a system of closure, but the desire for openness which is found in those moments when the world is experienced as a mysterious and wonderful place.'[74] What religion does, explains Lawson, is 'draw our attention to the limitation of our everyday understanding and to point to that which is not understood, to that which lies beyond closure.'[75]

Lawson describes superbly the dialogue inherent in religion: the complete picture versus the incomplete. Faith versus uncertainty. Speech versus the ineffable. Submission to doctrine versus free exploration. The dialogue he describes is one to have within oneself, as well as with others. What is attractive about Lawson is that the language he uses is indeterminate: religion 'draws our attention to'; religion 'points'. Religion, in its quest for openness, does not declare, assert, persuade. It cannot do so, and those that challenge its very existence (e.g. Richard Dawkins) wrestle merely with that aspect of a 'closed' religion – which is culturally bound and exoteric – and do not even touch what is the genuine core of religion, the willingness to submit to what one does not understand.

In the same way as he does with religion, Lawson distinguishes between art which is 'closed' – mere illustration which has a defined function within a book, crafts *et cetera* – and the ability of true art to transport, to take the viewer to another place of which he is uncertain. The other arts function in the same way: 'The deliberate avoidance of closure serves the same function in a text as it does in a painting, the search for openness through the avoidance of closure can be the defining characteristic of literary art … a text can also seek to avoid closure … by providing levels of meaning that cannot be fully deciphered.'[76]

Lawson is describing a knowledge of truth unlike any other, and he does so without using either the word 'knowledge' or 'truth'. He does not beg questions. He does not invite analyses. He rather describes the layered psychological process of how human beings *come to know*.

To go back, then, to the poem *Stopping by Woods on a Snowy Evening*, how is it that we 'know' what the poem is about? The word 'death' is never mentioned. More magically, death is not even implied by the vocabulary used. There is no gloom and doom, rather, *The woods are lovely, dark and deep*. A child would not understand the poem. Taken literally, the poem is about an inviting view that cannot be indulged owing to pressure of time.

But, I suggest, we, its adult readers, *intuit the sublimity of the moment*, and sublimity can be defined as 'breaking forth into absolute openness.' We recognize the moment because of experiences of our own that we have never verbalized. We had prior *knowledge*, even though we did not know we had that knowledge, and indeed, if we had known we had that knowledge the poem would not have worked for us so well. We would have had the poem tagged and logged; 'closed' in Lawson's terminology, and to that extent would not have felt moved by it. Art and religion work on us by breaking through closure, and our experience of the sublime happens at that very moment of breaking through.

Lawson never actually mentions the concept of sublimity in his work, but the literature in my first chapter – which locates the sublime as the effect of something other than us, which is infinite and unknowable, on our very souls – chimes exactly with Lawson's words:

> Human desire can be regarded as an outcome of the complex layered system of closure that realizes our experience. We desire openness because the move towards openness allows for the continuance of the process of closure. As a result, in the same way that the realization of closure can be experienced as desirable, so also can we find desirable the absence of closure. It is, to use familiar

examples, a feeling we can sense under the stars on a dark night, or facing out to sea as a storm develops. A sense of the immensity that cannot be captured through closure. An awareness of the inexplicable, of the failure of closure, and in that moment a sense that there is something deeper in the abandonment of closure than in the habitual framework that surrounds us. Some of our deepest feelings are thereby associated with the absence of closure. In silence and stillness, in the abandonment of the here and now. Not the moment of closure but the moment in its wake.[77]

There is no entry for 'sublime' in Lawson's index: the feeling remains suitably untagged.

A Possible Place for the Sublime in Kant's Epistemology

The difference between Kant and modern analytic philosophers is that he does not dismiss the subjective out of hand; rather he incorporates subjective truth into the very body of what it is to possess knowledge, and almost at the very top of Kant's metaphysical pyramid what he calls 'a priori synthetic knowledge' will reign. He even gives mathematics this status. It is synthetic, rather than analytic, *on account of its human input*. And it is *a priori*, rather than *a posteriori*, because such knowledge would remain knowledge in all possible worlds. Thus he puts man's sensibilities at the centre of the universe. There is no 'mere' here: when Kant argues that time and space are 'intuitions', he is not thereby dismissing some sure foundation of real knowledge. He is saying that man cannot come to know anything except through the medium of time and space.

Subjective understanding is, Kant repeatedly tells us, more than human psychology. He even talks about a special 'harmony' between the capacities of the knower and the nature of the known. But if his 'noumena' are unknowable by reason, and 'understanding' can only give us answers in the practical realm, how is mere intuition to be substantiated? How is subjectivity to be given objectivity? What 'faculty' or 'power' are we using? His answer is 'judgement', which he sees as being the mid-point between 'reason' and 'understanding'. But perhaps his answer is wrong; certainly, he will find he is stuck with all his old problems. For how can a reflective judgement which is 'indeterminate' take place without a prior concept?

His answers to the question won't satisfy him, to the extent that near the end of the third Critique he raises the possibility of an *intellectus archtypus*, or 'architectonic understanding', on which Douglas Burnham writes:

> Such an understanding would not function in a world of appearances, but directly in the world of things-in-themselves. Its power of giving the universal (concepts and ideas) would not be a separate power from its power of forming intuitions of particular things; concept and thing, thought and reality would be one.[78]

Kant seems to be invoking something akin to Pseudo-Dionysius' *aitia* – the ultimate 'cause' or 'ground' which is unknowable and of which nothing can be predicated. (See chapter three). We are also reminded of the 'common root' he is seeking between imagination and reason.

I want to suggest in this essay that the real connection he might have made is between his 'noumena' (placed, even more determinedly, beyond the law, beyond the known) and the 'sublime feeling within us', the one mirroring the other between two worlds.

He wrote his third Critique, I believe, not to give us a reputable and persuasive theory of aesthetics, but to restore the God he had so successfully annihilated in his First Critique. The stars above and the moral law within: these were what drove him.

Other Interpretations of the Sublime in Kant: Aesthetics versus Epistemology

Commentators on Kant's theory can be divided into those who want to see it 'bounded' (the aestheticians), and those who are looking for something more, something epistemological.

Kirk Pillow is an aesthetician. He takes issue with postmodern treatments of the sublime that proclaim its 'ineluctable alterity, violence and negativity'[79] and emphasizes 'the positive role of a sublime understanding in the interpretative manufacture of always partial, never shared worlds.'[80] Pillow uses aspects of Kant's theory and aligns it both with Kant's account of beauty and Hegel's aesthetic theory. He is one of those who like to quote:

> The beautiful in nature concerns the form of the object, which consists in (the object's) being bounded. But the sublime can also be found in a formless object, insofar as we present unboundedness, either in the object or because the object prompts us to present it, while yet we add to this unboundedness the thought of its totality.[81]

Pillow wants it to be possible for the sublime to exist in an object with form, and the word 'also' excites him. He quotes Rudolf Makkreel in his observation that 'Kant does not write that the sublime can be found *only* in a formless object, but that it can *also* be found there.'[82] And despite Kant referring explicitly to nature, Pillow insists that 'the same bound/unbound distinction applies to the work of art as well.'[83] This might be true, but Kant famously loved nature and was famously indifferent to works of art, and my feeling is that Pillow is using Kant against Kant's will. For again and again (see Chapter one), Kant makes the claim that 'the sublime cannot be contained in any sensuous form', we just think so because of an act of 'subreption', and it is the feeling which the object induces which 'is itself sublime – sublime because the mind had been incited to abandon sensibility and employ itself upon ideas involving higher finality.'[84]

Jeremy Gilbert-Rolfe is also keen to incorporate the sublime into an account of beauty. His conclusions are even more dramatic. He sees a role for the sublime in 'squaring up infinity':

> announcing its control of the infinite through its division or formation into a grid. Thus, in the genealogy of technology, from the Cartesian grid, to Leibniz and continuity made out of points, to the television and computer, reconvening within and through the mathematical a force like life's but independent of it.[85]

I would suggest, however, that Kant's theory of the sublime does not want to go here, and will not follow us into the room where the TV stands (even if it is framed by a Derridean 'parergon'.) Far more fruitful and faithful to the spirit of Kant is an interpretation by Robert Clewis.

Clewis' book is called *The Kantian Sublime and the Revelation of Freedom.* Freedom is an extremely important concept for Kant: without it, morality is meaningless, Kant argues – moral decisions are made by the 'supersensible self' which is over and above nature. In other words, our self-consciousness is clue to that freedom. Clewis writes:

> In the experience of the sublime, as we have just seen, the imagination is given a task by reason but fails to complete it. Since the imagination falls short, the activity of the imagination is characterized as serious (KU5:245). While this failure is frustrating for the imagination, it has at least two positive effects. In failing, the imagination feels itself

enlarged or raised up (KU 5:249, 262, 269). This extension counts as a type of freedom. That is, the imagination feels a kind of freedom in trying to complete the task given to it by reason. Second, the imagination's failure reveals the presence of the faculty of reason. Although the imagination fails, it is in harmony with reason in promoting reason's aims (KU5:244). Thus, the failure of the imagination allows the subject to become aware of his or her transcendence or transcendental freedom. The imagination serves the interests of reason through its sacrifice by making the mind aware of its rational superiority to sensibility.[86]

What is attractive about Clewis's arguments is the prominent position held by *revelation* in his description of how the sublime works upon us. In his discussion on the unbounded nature of the sublime, he is happy to accept (unlike Pillow) Kant's account of 'subreption' – namely, that the sublime exists in us rather than in an object.

In Clewis' interpretation, something has happened to the subject; he feels his imagination raised up, he is conscious of freedom. His imagination cannot complete the task given by reason, so there is further revelation: the presence of the faculty of reason. Most gloriously of all, the subject becomes aware of 'his or her transcendental freedom'. Clewis complains that Lyotard uses the notion of Kant's sublime as 'a sign of the heterogeneous differend', but that the sublime's 'heterogeneousness' is downplayed to merely being a part of another language game. He says:

> For Lyotard, the transition is not from nature to freedom, but from a family of propositions to another family of propositions. Moving in this way is like crossing a large body of water, skipping from island to island, led by the faculty of judgment's navigational skills. 'Each family of propositions would be, as it were, like an island.' There is little mention here of an end, much less a moral one. Lyotard fails to interpret the Kantian sublime as a revelation of human freedom.'[87]

But if Lyotard fails to see the full potential of Kant's theory, so does Kant himself. On the one hand he makes an attempt to schematize the sublime: he talks of the 'supersensible employment' of the 'sensible in nature', revealing (subjectively) the 'absolutely good' which works on the subject by means of 'an absolutely necessitating law' and involves 'not a mere claim, but a command upon every one to assent, and belongs intrinsically not to the aesthetic but to the pure intellectual judgement.'[88] But how does this sit with his earlier comments, that the sublime is 'ill-adapted to our faculty of presentation' and 'an outrage on the imagination',[89] and that it is nature's 'chaos' and 'its wildest and most irregular disorder and desolation'[90] which excite the sublime?

Kant is a systematic metaphysician; that's what he does for a living, as it were. He once called this his 'public life' in contrast to his 'private life', in which he included anxieties about money *et cetera*. But Kant, in his quest for schematic perfection, neglected the full potential of a theory that might have brought his public and private lives together. He is spiritually attracted to what he does not know, but in public, he sets himself the task of solving his 'antimonies'. How is one to be profoundly subjective and objective at one and the same time? In public, he never solves it; but in private, his knowledge that such a thing is possible is absolute.

Conclusion

In trying to locate the indeterminate, Hilary Lawson is Kant's natural successor; but the difference between them is that Lawson unconditionally embraces openness as a means to new knowledge, whereas Kant is anxious, at least publicly, to bound unboundedness.

Art and religion are vehicles that break through accounts of scientific knowledge: they do indeed require a judgment that is 'reflective' and 'indeterminate'. But the kind of knowledge such judgment yields cannot be captured by Kant's metaphysical project as it stands, and perhaps it's not even 'judgment' he's after, *but a different way of knowing altogether.* The paradox remains: what is made known in art and religion, a spiritual reality, remains unknown. It cannot be pinned down or tagged, and the moment it is, the moment its mystery is taken from it, it loses that very quality it engenders in the observer. When

Holman Hunt's picture of Christ lighting the way was first exhibited, it moved people. When it was hung in every house in Victorian England, it became emblematic, commonplace, while knowledge of what is truly other is eternally new and authentic. By its very nature, it is incommunicable. The knowledge is a-linguistic: it is more of a recognition, or if there is a word at all, that word is 'yes'.

But if we inhabit one world and 'the other' another, how are we to describe our relationship to that world? Why is it, even, that we suspect such a relationship exists at all? Kant suggests that the peasant from Savoyard does not have a relationship with the sublime because his soul is untutored in morality, while the lords and ladies of court will have a sense of it because the indeterminate nature of the sublime will reveal the determinacy of their own natures, which are subject to the moral law.[91] Though Kant's example might be off the mark, his sense of a journey towards truth being marked by a dialectic between the determinate and the indeterminate, each revealing the other, seems (intuitively) correct.

Why it is, however, that Lawson's chosen words, 'closure' and 'openness' express the event more accurately than Kant's (though ultimately expressing the same event) is because 'closure' and 'openness' express the *attitude* of a human being towards what is outside of himself. *Closure* and *openness* are psychological rather than philosophical terms, they are more about *us* than about what is out there. Kant himself locates the sublime in us, and not in the indeterminate: the indeterminate is merely the catalyst that reveals to us who we are.

The sublime is what is ultimately indecipherable. It is beyond even intuition, because intuition immediately demands a content and there is no content. The sublime is no-thing, but affects us nonetheless, to the extent of revealing our own humanity.

The relationship we have with the sublime cannot be described as 'knowledge' in the ordinary sense, nor even intuition, by which I mean knowledge without reason, without language. It is more a radical confrontation with something utterly other. The German word *Sehnsucht* manages to convey the peculiar combination of fear and longing involved. When we lose ourselves the subject becomes one with its object. There is simply no room for anything more. It is the place where we as persons are momentarily lost. It is a place of radical freedom, where there are no signposts.

Anthony Monti wants the 'other' to have content – beauty, truth, God *et cetera*, and if his reasoning suggests art and religion work in the same way in how they transport us there (by means of metaphor, literally 'a carrying beyond') I am extremely sympathetic to it. But this fleshing out of the 'other' is not necessary. His account is not violent enough, for want of a better word. Revelation is shocking. It snatches you from the familiar, like it or not, will it or not. But my argument is this: the sublime reveals to us who we are and what we need without a single word being spoken or written.

Chapter Three

Post-Modernism, Negative Theology and the Sublime

Introduction

As I have shown in the previous chapter, new knowledge happens at the borderline between closure and openness. There is a confrontation between what is received and understood and what is still to be received and understood, a confrontation which may or may not be resolved. In art, a new movement requires a new way of seeing, a shock out of an old way of seeing. Both classical and romantic movements took hundreds of years to evolve; but with the advent of photography and the question, 'Why is art different from pure representation?', that difference was explored again and again in quick succession, with each new movement designed to wake the seer from his old pre-suppositions and take him *somewhere else*. The impressionists and expressionists convinced Tolstoy that art was about 'self-expression'; but modern conceptual artists such as Marcel Duchamp were keen to show that there was no definition of art which was an absolute, that one could find a 'readymade': a bicycle wheel or a bottlerack, a 'work of art without an artist to make it', and by means of a signature and a title ('Bicycle-wheel', 'Bottlerack') re-classify the object as art.[92]

I would argue that post-modernism as a movement is *analogous* to an encounter with the sublime, i.e. what is radically *other*. It involves a rupture with the very fabric of our knowing. Post-modernists, once assumed to be the heralds of a new atheistic age, have, on closer inspection, sympathy with 'negative' theology as propounded by mystics such as Pseudo-Dionysius and Meister Eckhart. In this chapter I shall

a) Look at why post-modernism has been such a bone of contention in the modern academic world.

b) Show how Derrida might have more in common with the great mystical theologians than he admits to.

c) Conclude by suggesting that the borderline between the known and the unknown constitutes a 'rupture', and that it is in this rupture that the experience of the sublime resides.

A Critique of Post-modernism

Post-modernism is a reaction to modernity. It is radically iconoclastic, breaking down the old certainties (for what did they bring us? The godforsaken twentieth century) and no academic discipline or cultural movement has escaped its rage. There is no formal definition, and its parameters are ever shifting, but as post-modernism resists legalistic language and would only knock down what would then become 'another movement with its own certainties', its ability to have evaded definition is surely to its advantage. But its central tenet has been Derrida's *il n'y a pas de hors-texte,* or, 'there is no 'outside-text' – meaning that a text can only look back at itself to acquire validity, and therefore all 'texts' are equally valid. Derrida describes, rightly, how the implicit truth criterion of language has been 'the face of God';[93] but with no God, there is no truth. Language, therefore, depends on *différance* for its meaning: every word is haunted by its antonym, its other: it is the inter-textual *contrast* between words which makes language work as a communicating medium; but there is no 'truth' out there which gives some texts more validity than others.

Post-modernism is therefore intrinsically disturbing. It accuses, after all, those who would see themselves as dispassionate seekers after truth as 'committed to dominant ideologies'. It is quick to accuse us of making 'value-judgements', not just intentionally but in everything we say, and indeed there is no 'I' over and above the 'discourse' in which we find ourselves locked in. And rather like the state disappearing in the last stages of the ideal communist society, the author of post-modern tracts must herself disappear into the very discourse that she has tried to look 'objectively' upon.

Unsurprisingly, then, 'reactionary' academics have abhorred post-modernism. Anthony Monti was spurred to write *A Natural Theology of the Arts* (2003) as an attempt to defeat its conclusions. He writes in his introduction, under the heading, 'Addressing the Crisis in the Humanities':

> Whatever else may be said of postmodernist trends, therefore, they share one crucial feature: a tendency to question the very notion of an original, independent truth or reality to which the arts, morality, or indeed any kind of 'discourse' could refer. No wonder, then, that as Peter Fuller observes, 'Postmodernism knows no commitments.'[94]

Likewise, the social anthropologist Ernest Gellner is passionate in his own tirade against post-modernism. Having acknowledged that the starting-point of post-modernists was to raise a reasonable doubt, 'namely that there are tools used in knowledge, and that these deserve and require examination', and that they were right to ask the question whether there might be any link between such tools and 'the indisputable fact that there is in this world a great deal of inequality of power', to the extent that they actually '*make* the worlds which they claim to *find*', Gellner is infuriated by their conclusions:

> Unfortunately, members of the movement jump to conclusions a little too fast, with a tendency to answer the question by a facile Yes (to qualify the answer is to confess oneself a reactionary) and then, in an ambivalent attempt to find a way out of the relativist impasse, become evermore enmeshed in a regress in which nothing is allowed to stand,

or everything stands and falls equally. They rather like this impasse, it constitutes their speciality, their distinction, their superiority over the poor benighted objectivists.[95]

There are other scholars, however, who positively greet Postmodernism, who not only respond to the challenges it poses but dance on the ashes of the *ancien regime*. In *Mysticism after Modernity,* Don Cupitt declares:

> There is no First Principle: everything is secondary. Just the streaming, purely contingent flux of things, unpoliced, is well able to generate natural languages, values, organisms, and human societies. Relativity is creativity: the world is just *play*. The mysticism of secondariness accepts universal pure contingency, goes with the flow, and trusts the processes of life spontaneously to generate forms and meaning. Let it come. And – it does! Not by Reason and skill, but by contingency and play. Let it be: let the world make itself. Relativity and play are highly creative, whereas 'absolutes' create nothing. Absolutes are utterly useless. They are sterile.[96]

If Cupitt construes the absolute as a thing, and his grammar suggests that he does, he is right, of course. But the absolute is not a rule, a text, a place. The absolute is ever-moving, like a dance which invites us to join in. You don't hold a dance, you perform it, you enter into it, and you don't see it in its entirety until you leave the stage and remember it, and then you only have the trace.

I find Cupitt's tone to be more angry than playful: there's no certainty of anything, so the First Principle be damned, and isn't that great, we can play like creative children and do just as we please! John Caputo, meanwhile, is both mesmerizing and affirming in his use of language. He writes:

> I am simply saying, or confessing, in a kind of post-modern Augustinian confession, that we do not know who we are – to which I hasten to add: and *that* is who we are. We are not thereby left with nothing but rather with ourselves, with the *questio mihi factus sum.* We are left holding the bag – of our *passion,* the passion of our not-knowing, our passion for God, of our love of God, when we do not know what we love when we love our God.[97]

Caputo is surely right. Faith is not about embracing certainties, assenting to a set of propositions. 'Love of God' is something passionately felt. Caputo writes:

> Contrary to what a good many ortho-religious people think, people who are rightly attached to the particular figures and symbols and propositions by which they have been formed, *we do not know what we believe or to whom we are praying.*[98]

Religious feeling is a leap in the dark, but above all it is *feeling*. Caputo calls it a 'leap of love to the hyper-real'. And note that it is *feeling* rather than cold-blooded reason that has been the impetus both behind post-modernism in the first place, and such violent and heart-felt responses to it.

Derrida and Negative Theology

Derrida's method is more one of a performance artist than an academic. If Kant's most sublime utterance is inscribed on the Temple of Isis, 'I am all that has been and all that will be and no mortal has seen my face', Derrida is the resident Temple dancer with the veils. For the project of deconstruction is not simply to add more texts to the great pile of texts 'to be deconstructed', but rather to suggest, tantalize, provoke and play with his readers, keeping each point that he makes nimble and light on its feet, ready to be dissolved by the merest breath. So to the academics who solemnly pore over his works, hungry for some consistent thesis, he complains that he has not been 'read well enough'; and to Jack Caputo, who chaired a dialogue between him and Jean-Luc Marion on the subject of 'The Gift' – once Derrida's signature tune where he asks, what part does power play in the act of giving? – he says the subject now bores him and he hasn't much thought of it for ten years.

Academics are trained to look at texts rather than the personalities that produce them. I have suggested in my first chapter that Kant, despite his demolition of exclusively rational proofs for the existence of God, is actually looking for the space wherein God might reside – apparent from remarks off the cuff, as it were, rather than within the main body of his

Critiques. In his theory of the sublime, he over-schematizes, he wants a snug fit with his first two Critiques. But he is so close to the answer he is looking for, so succinctly put by Hilary Lawson, whose theory of closure and openness draws on Kant to build a theory of his own. Meanwhile, Derrida does not want to schematize, he abhors and distrusts schematization. If Kant is prone to fore-close, as in closing down before he needs to, Derrida is prone to keeping open every single avenue, to *never* reduce 'knowledge' to bite-sized chunks, digestible by all. He keeps it all irresistibly open. Or perhaps it is closer to the truth to say that he closes down everyone else's avenue (*'il n'y a pas de hors-texte'*; or, 'no meaning can be determined out of context, but no context permits saturation')[99] while resolutely refusing to let others second-guess him. The man who once said, 'I rightly pass for an atheist' never stands still on the deeper questions, but poses rather as Apollo himself.

Kevin Hart makes some attempt to rein him in in *Post-Secular Philosophy*. He quotes from Derrida's *Circumfession* (1993), where he writes of his:

Religion about which nobody understands anything, any more than does my mother who asked other people a while ago, not daring to talk to me about it, if I still believed in God ... but she must have known that the constancy of God in my life is called by other names, so that I quite rightly pass for an atheist, the omnipresence to me of what I call God in my absolved, absolutely private language being neither that of an eyewitness nor that of a voice doing anything other than talking to me without saying anything.[100]

As Hart remarks, 'Scarcely a declaration of faith, this expression is also not a straightforward affirmation of atheism.' What a game Derrida plays with us! His play with religious language: 'circumfession', 'omnipresence', 'absolved'; his religion which is so 'private' (though he has no belief in private languages), and above all, the 'voice doing anything other than talking to me without saying anything.'

Derrida's language is reminiscent of the poetry of e.e. cummings. And yet, it does go somewhere, we *want* it to go somewhere. Elsewhere, in a meditation on Antonin Artaud, he writes, 'The death of God will ensure our salvation because the death of God alone can reawaken the Divine,' and even, 'The divine has been ruined by God.' Suddenly, we have Meister Eckhart himself speaking, with his distinction between 'God' ('To say that God is good is to do him wrong: as well say that the sun is black.')[101] and the Godhead beyond God.

What is interesting to me is that both Kant and Derrida had mothers to whom religious faith was important, and they were both close to them. Even Derrida seems to have believed in God as a child. In both, therefore, at bottom, there will be a sense of yearning, even if that yearning is for a faith lost. Yet, in the same way as Kant demolishes arguments for the existence of God, Derrida comes down hard on all who look for some sense of the 'beyond'.

Derrida's interpretation of Kant's sublime, is, not surprisingly, to bring it down to the realm of ordinary discourse. Because the imagination fails to comprehend the concept 'infinity', it can only be 'bounded' by the 'unbounded' power of reason: hence the 'parergon' framing the 'ergon', and hence bringing the 'ergon' as 'ergon' into existence. It is the setting of limits that gives rise to the pleasure experienced in the sublime, not in the surrender of those limits. In fact, I think Kant would have liked Derrida's interpretation, when he was in a certain mood. But it seems to me that both Kant and Derrida have failed to see the potential of the sublime in a theory of knowledge. Even Pseudo-Dionysius and Jean-Luc Marion fail to persuade Derrida that negative theology – at least the negative theology of others besides himself – is actually another name for the metaphysics of presence.

Derrida's complaint against negative theology is that it is 'always occupied with letting a superessential reality go beyond finite categories of essence and existence, that is, of presence, and always hastens to remind us that, if we deny the predicate of existence to God, it is in order to recognize him as a superior, inconceivable and ineffable mode of Being.'[102] Derrida's tone is irritated, and it is, to my mind, irritating. It is as though he were saying, 'Deconstruction is the only religion here! I travel to what is truly *impossible*. I say *oui, oui, viens, viens* to what is *tout autre*, and everyone else is just pretending, by using paradoxical expressions for 'presence'.'

Derrida is right at a very simple level. It is one thing to say, 'This is a beautiful hat', and actually, something very similar is being said if you deny it, 'This is not just a beautiful hat, it is beyond beauty.' The word 'ineffably' has come to mean little more than 'very'. Derrida argues in his own thesis, *Sauf le Nom,* that he is the one that goes beyond feeding the expectations of Christian Neoplatonists, he is the one who is going to 'Save the Name' (of God) for everyone! Caputo explains:

> So if Derrida and Marion are two apostles of the impossible, Derrida is a more Pauline figure, who wants all the *gentiles,* the *goyim,* to share in the good news, while Marion is more Petrine and insistent on a straiter gate.[103]

And what is Derrida's magic formula, that preserves the other as truly other? *Tout autre est tout autre,* he proclaims. Is he really saying something 'other' himself?

There seems to me to be a parallel here between Derrida's criticisms of negative theology (your 'nothing' is really a 'something') and Lawson's criticisms of Kant's *noumena* (by even naming something nameless and unknowable, you are relinquishing openness in favour of 'closure'), and in the work of both Derrida and Lawson they are anxious to avoid words which in any way define an 'end-point': 'openness' is left absolutely open, because the moment it becomes a possibility, it disappears, or rather is absorbed into all other possibilities, and, as Caputo is fond of remarking (after Climacus) 'the possible is a mediocre fellow'. What both Lawson and Derrida are happy to express, however, is the *feeling* which accompanies looking into what is unremittingly open or 'impossible'; while Lawson prefers the vocabulary of the sublime: 'a feeling we can sense under the stars on a dark night, or facing out to sea as a storm develops ... an awareness of the inexplicable, of the failure of closure, and in that moment a sense that there is something deeper in the abandonment of closure than in the habitual framework that surrounds us',[104] Derrida's deconstruction goes like this:

> A call for the coming of something unforeseeable and unprogrammable, a call that is nourished by the expectation of something to *come*, structurally to come, for which we pray and weep, sigh and dream. Deconstruction is (like) a deep desire for a Messiah who never shows (up), a subtle spirit or elusive spectre that would be extinguished by the harsh hands of presence and actuality.[105]

I would argue that both Lawson and Derrida are looking at the sublime, albeit in their idiosyncratic ways, with Lawson's emphasis on the present and Derrida's on 'what is to come'. Returning to Frost's poem, there is both an *awareness* of and a *yearning* for sublimity. The deep dark woods are not sublime in themselves but *promise sublimity*, they promise *tout autre*.

But my point in this essay is to suggest that the mileage in a theory of the sublime, or openness, or *tout autre* is not as an ontology but as an epistemology. Whether negative theology is talking about what is *really* something or *really* nothing is beside the point. For the sublime is not a thing but a function, a verb with no reference. Kant's theory gets so far, but doesn't quite clinch it. His theory certainly captures the 'astonishment' involved in an encounter with the sublime, we have the 'outrage on the imagination', but he doesn't make explicit that its *very lack of boundedness* is what *reveals* to us our own *boundedness.* It is through our confrontation with the sublime that we come to know ourselves.

Jean-Luc Marion quotes from Nicholas de Cusa in his paper 'In the Name':

> According to negative theology, infinity is all we discover in God. This infinity does not revert to affirmation after passing through negation, but lays bare and circumscribes the divine truth as the experience of incomprehension.[106]

The Latin word for 'lay bare' is *lucere*, to light up, to reveal. Infinity, that without form, *has the function of revelation,* and what infinity reveals is *praecisionem veritatis*, literally, the 'precision of truth': a sense of truth is sharpened by gazing upon infinity. Is this not consistent with Kant's observations on the sublime? In Kant, the 'precision of truth' is within ourselves, in the recognition of the moral law, in the sense that, ultimately, we are the victors over the most raging tempest. And that faculty was *planted in us* by our creator. For Nicholas de Cusa, I would argue, the feeling would be equally sublime.

Marion also quotes extensively from Pseudo-Dionysius'
Mystical Theology. What Marion is looking for is a third way
(with which to enchant the recalcitrant Derrida), which 'is
played out beyond the oppositions between affirmation and
negation, synthesis and separation, in short between true and
false.'[107] Pseudo-Dionysius uses the same vocabulary. He looks
'beyond every affirmation and negation' and 'beyond every
privation':

> Neither one nor oneness, neither divinity nor goodness, nor
> spirit in the sense we understand it; neither sonship nor
> fatherhood, nor anything else that is known by us or by any
> of the other beings ... we cannot even speak of God as
> goodness, the most revered of names ... He who is praised
> manifoldly with a manifold of names, is called by the
> Scriptures ineffable and anonymous.[108]

Marion makes the point that a manifold of names reduces the
one so named to anonymity: names stop working as names.
And to 'He who surpasses all nomination' Pseudo-Dionysius
gives the title *aitia*, or 'ground' which, according to Marion, 'has
no other function but to pass beyond every affirmation and
negation':

> *aitia* in no way names God; it de-nominates him by
> suggesting the strictly pragmatic function of language –
> namely to refer names and their speaker to the unattainable
> yet inescapable interlocutor beyond every name and every

denegation of names. With *aitia*, speech does not say any more than it denies – it acts by transporting itself in the direction of Him whom it denominates.[109]

Language has been seen in this essay as a hurdle to truth; how does language latch on to the world? As soon as it does, there is closure and we can communicate 'what we know' to each other; but it is in openness, in the incomprehensible (because we do not have the language as yet to filter it, comprehend it, categorize it) where 'truth' is revealed, *praecisionem veritatis*. But now what Marion does is to elevate the language that is neither a 'Proper Name' *nor* a predicate; he suggests that some language is *beyond* the logic of predication, some language we just *do* as in prayer and praise, which has an arrow and is directed but has no content as such. He says, 'prayer definitively marks the transgression of the predicative, nominative, and therefore metaphysical sense of language.'[110] It's like shouting 'Hallelujah!' Language escapes being language. And despite Derrida's analytic suspicion of the 'third way', he fully embraces the ability of language to shake off it chains, and indeed, on being asked by Marion to make explicit his views on negative theology, he writes:

(43) Now I think that if time permitted I could show that my texts on the subject are written texts, by which I mean that they are not a thesis on a theme. They have a pragmatic aspect, a performative aspect that would require another kind of analysis.[111]

This is extraordinary. Derrida spent his life 'exposing' texts, revealing them to have been written (unconsciously, of course) not in the spirit of Socrates (who sought 'Justice Itself') but in that of Thrasymachus (Justice is always in the interests of the stronger). He reduced metaphysics to dust with his steely scalpel; but then, having beaten the opposition, so to speak, he seems to have joined them. (Caputo even suggests that the Messiah he is waiting for is 'Justice'.) Derrida performs too; he dances, he teases, he invites, and then turns away. Derrida is doing something akin to art. And like the artist, who is ultimately egotistical, he will have no truck with the 'third way' as propounded by Marion, Dionysius, Eckhart *et cetera*, because he wants his own third way. Caputo calls him an 'Apostle of the Impossible': I would suggest he sees himself more as a High Priest.

Yet he shares with Meister Eckhart not only a paradoxical style, but a good deal of common ground. Eckhart distinguishes "God" who is part of the world from the "Godhead" who is the radically other – the *tout autre* of Derrida. How does one reach him?

> Whoever is seeking God by ways is finding ways and losing God, who in ways is hidden. But whoever is seeking God without ways will find him as he is in himself.[112]

In ordinary discourse we won't get there, in other words, we have to make a leap into the *tout autre*. We have to break through somewhere else.

> But when I enter the ground, the bottom, the flood and source of the Godhead, no one asks me where I come from or where I have been. There no one misses me, and God 'unbecomes'.[113]

Eckhart is describing a place where language, even the word "God", doesn't work anymore.

Derrida never concedes that negative theology succeeds in negating its negation, and always accuses it as a project whose hidden agenda is to say 'Yes! Three times, yes!' But if he had looked more carefully at what Eckhart actually writes, he would notice that he is far from being playful about these core themes of being and non-being; rather he builds his meta-metaphysics on the very building-block of the negation of negation.

Eckhart is a dialectician, and for dialectic to work there has to be an absolute difference between the thesis and antithesis. Two poles have to crash up against each other to produce a third entity. In Eckhart's case, the two poles (remarkably) are the creator and his creation. Edward Howell makes the point that 'Creation is, then, apparently not part of Eckhart's spiritual path, excluded by its complete otherness from God.'[114] And yet, and this is the point, this is how the dialectic works, 'We need creation to get us to God, but only to show us what God is not.' Howell writes:

> Creation, in this view, has only a negative role in spirituality, as something to be negated in order to make progress. One

could add that Eckhart also speaks of creation positively. He does not always say that creation is nothing. But in this case, he simply reverses the polarity of the negation, saying that if creation is something, then God is nothing.[115]

Having established these poles, then, Eckhart goes a stage further (and indeed without it his theology would come to an impasse). This is the negation of negation. What Eckhart would say (himself drawing on Pseudo-Dionysius) is that the statement 'Creation and the creator are opposites' is located in creation and therefore has to be denied, because it cannot be the truth. Negation belongs to creation. Eckhart says, in German Sermon 21:

> All creatures have a negation in themselves; one creature denies that it is the other creature … But God has a negation of negation; he is one and negates everything other, for outside God is nothing … By negating something of God, I catch hold of something he is *not*. It is precisely this that has to be removed. God is one, he is a negation of negation.

In other words, creatures belong in the world of language, where to 'deny' is the function of a word. What is beyond affirmation and denial turns out to be radically other. In Eckhart's dialectic, the war of words 'creation' and 'creator' spawns the 'ground', the *aitia*. The third way turns out to be as close to Derrida's *tout autre* as it can conceivably be.

Conclusion

Rupture:
A theory of the sublime

The sublime is not something that we make a gentle progress towards; the sublime is not a journey or something which can be willed. The sublime is *rupture* from all the comforting, familiar aspects of our existence, and from language itself. The sublime takes us from ourselves to what is radically other, and then returns us to ourselves as new, enhanced beings, conscious not so much that we are rational (in the sense of being able to do mathematics) but of what is 'super-sensible' within us. In Kant's scheme he asks too much: he wants our 'reason' to be activated into 'respect' of the 'moral law'; or perhaps he asks too little, when what he is wanting to say (and occasionally dares to) is what we are apprehending when our feelings are at their most sublime is 'God'.

The literal translation of *sublimis* is 'high, exalted'. But a theory of the sublime in which 'the sublime' was reduced to 'exalted things' would not have had the depth I require of it.

Artists and poets of the seventeenth and eighteenth centuries had a vague and romantic idea of something irresistibly other, which was some 'higher force'. But Virgil's 'other shore' is not higher, it is just 'other'; and my theory suggests it is so radically other, so beyond Being itself (which belongs to this world of creation) that we would not recognize it if we saw it and only know it by the trace it leaves.

Burke remarks in the preface of the second edition of his *Philosophical Enquiry* that the word 'sublime' is less important than the reality behind that word. I would suggest, therefore, that in this essay I have invoked a diverse range of supporters, whether they actually use the word 'sublime' or not: Lawson, Derrida, Marion, Eckhart. I would further suggest that the great artist is more than a great craftsman: he is the enhanced self that looks out onto the incomprehensible, wherein *praecisionem veritatis* is revealed, and which he, in turn, reveals to us. The making of art is about the journey between what is known and unknown and back again; and religion shares that journey, religion *risks* that journey.

Post-modernism is also about the yearning for rupture, because without rupture there can be no escape. There needs to be a naming beyond naming, a 'de-nomination'. There has to be a 'hyper-real'. There even has to be a gift beyond the gift, because otherwise the giver and the recipient of the gift remain permanently in deadlock, the power of the giver remaining tantalizingly equal to the value of the gift. Caputo suggests a resolution:

In order to give a gift, we must give in to that aporia but without giving up. With the madness of father Abraham himself atop Mount Moriah, we must, dagger in hand, tear up the circle of time and the debt and plunge into the impossible, *doing* what is impossible, going where we cannot go.

That moment of madness is the time of the gift. That is why Derrida can say he has spent his whole life 'inviting calling, promising, hoping, sighing, dreaming.' Of the gift, of justice, of hospitality, of the incoming of the wholly other, of *the* impossible.[116]

Derrida is dreaming of rupture from the possible. He wants to break out, and take us with him. For some, he is the Messianic figure himself.

Caputo suggests that 'we must tear up the circle of time.' Clayton Crockett wants a rupture equally profound. In his concluding chapter, where he presents us with his 'theology of the sublime', he says:

'Thinking is living … if thinking broadly considered represents the possibility of life in general, the sublime marks a radical discontinuity or break which could be characterized as death. The sublime represents terrifying excess, loss of control, and in-breaking of imagination beyond the ability of reason and understanding to bring it to order …'[117]

This is heady stuff, but Crockett is not finished with us yet. He looks at the etymology of 're-flection' and sees it as 'bending back on itself'. The very activity of reflection, therefore, is a sort of rupture, and suggests that we might 'consider the sublime moment in thinking as a folding of form':

> This folding is the reflexivity of attempting to think that which is thinking. This activity, which is what makes thinking itself possible, also marks a disruption or a fissuring which is constitutive of subjectivity.[118]

This 'fissuring' Crockett sees as the task of theology, because, he says,

> This folding of form, of any particular norm of culture, testifies to a sublime moment which cannot be fully contained by the determinate form or image it takes. Theology for Tillich is then second-order reflection on religion, or the attempts to grapple with and understand this process, even as it evades all attempts to render it determinate and fully knowable.[119]

In other words absolute rupture, or 'fissure' in Crockett's words, is necessary in order to go beyond the 'determinate form' of a particular religion, and the sublime moment is integral to that rupture. He allies himself to Tillich again in his use of the word 'depth'. The 'depth' aspect of reason is the 'abyss', 'which must be understood in relation to the Kantian sublime, where the struggle between reason and imagination sets up a vibration which consists in "a rapid alternation of repulsion from, and attraction to, one and the same object".[120] Again, Crockett describes no peaceful, steady journey to God; the journey is broken, and the meeting is one of terrifying confrontation. Suddenly we are back with Burke all over again, where the self can only become one with its object *in terror*.

Crockett concludes his book with this final observation:

> A theology of the sublime, which is unable to be harnessed by reason towards moral ends, also resonates with a felt sense of disorientation, dizzying change, and the perceived breakdown of both social structures and patterns of thought.[121]

The sublime, as what is radically other, is what allows us to break free from any preconceptions, categories, boundaries we might have ever been brazen enough to have considered 'true'. It is by unknowing that we come to know. The story of Christ itself is one of rupture; of breaking free from the old ways, of breaking free, even, from death itself. All is possible. The now might just be eternal. As St Paul recommends, 'Do not be conformed to this aeon, but be transformed by the renewal of your mind.' (Rom. 12.2)

A Short Essay on Truth

'Truth' is an irresistible word; 'truthful' people are the ones we wish to make friends with, to marry, to be our Prime Minister. But it is just a word, and none of us can really say with any certainty what it refers to, or if it refers to anything much, or if it refers to everything, the whole shebang.

We have libraries of books with philosophers and logicians unravelling the complexities of the phrase, 'the cat sat on the mat', and then we have Keats, who tells us that 'truth is beauty, and beauty truth'. (A rhetorical flourish, I fear, but a nice try.) Then we have a film like *The Matrix* which tells us that truth might just be very far from beautiful, that we only *think* we are part of a real world, our minds are fed by a computer while our bodies are used as batteries to supply an alien lifeform with energy. The heroes want truth, though; they manage to unplug themselves from a comfortable illusion and see the devastated world for the bleak place it really is. And we, the audience, are right with them: our better selves would do the same.

In other words, human beings are driven to truth, no happy pills for us. In *The Gay Science*, Nietzsche calls it 'an unconditional will to truth' and a 'metaphysical faith'. We neither wish to deceive others, nor be deceived, and most importantly, we don't wish to deceive ourselves. We are ever alert to break through such deceptions.

It might seem that a philosophical account of language – what makes a statement true – and the more psychological account, what it is to live a 'true' life, a meaningful life which is lived with integrity, are two very different projects. My purpose in this short essay is to show how semantic meaning and psychological meaning are analogous. In the same way as a sentence requires a reference outside of itself in order to be properly meaningful, a life requires a reference outside of itself in order to be meaningful. A sentence must break through inter-referentiality; a good, 'literary' sentence through cliché, and a life lived authentically must break through mere convention and obedience to society's mores. Words, lives, both must be awake, as it were, in order to be significant.

In Greek, the word 'logos' means 'word' *and* 'reason' *and* 'meaning'. My ambition is to follow the Greeks and bring these three concepts under one umbrella. After all, a word has the task of dividing up reality in order to communicate – there is nothing intrinsically 'true' about a word, rather, it is the effectiveness of its representation that is the most important thing about it. The first verse in St John's gospel tells us that in the beginning was the 'Logos', and the 'Logos' was with God, and God was the 'Logos'. John goes on to *describe* a particular event in history with a universal meaning. He will do so by a series of propositions, each one of which might be deemed 'true' or 'false' (we weren't there and have no way of proving the veracity of any of the propositions). But we can evaluate its universal meaning. (In the ancient world 'meaning' and 'interpretation' was deemed significantly more important than the accurate reporting of historical events.)

In every language the nuance will be different, perhaps only accessible to the native speaker; indeed, in every sentence the nuance will be different, and serves as no more than a sorting-room between the speaker and the hearer, the space between them, as it were. To speak with accuracy is one difficulty; and to interpret correctly quite another. There's an American word used in the military and movies where a mission is orchestrated by ground control: 'copy', meaning 'understood'. In the military, a straightforward vocabulary and training makes 'copying' possible. Likewise, in the simple sentences used in everyday speech, such as 'leave the milk bottle by the door', 'copying' is the norm and makes everyday life possible. But when a speaker or writer's attempt at communication is more subtle, when emotions are discussed, or 'truth' indeed, the hearer/reader cannot 'copy', but recreates.

'Truth' will mean something different for the linguistic philosopher and those intent on seeking a psycho-religious meaning. In a correspondence theory of truth, a sentence is 'true' if it corresponds with reality; those who eschew correspondence will deem a sentence true when enough people think it is, a more pragmatic approach that might beg fewer questions, but ultimately the truth-value (if any) would be very slim indeed. Meanwhile, those who look for a psycho-religious meaning, will look not so much to a common language but a subjective experience. It remains indefinable/unverifiable but is nonetheless sufficiently universal among human beings past and present to be taken seriously. Most importantly, the sense of 'truth' for such people is more a *direction* rather than an *arrival*. We never get there, but the journey seems worthwhile.

So any preliminary definition of truth won't be an optimistic one. For the linguistic philosopher, it will be something like the sum of all true propositions, which, depending on your point of view, will either have to relate to reality or just be a coherent part of a language-game. For those seeking a grander concept of 'Truth' the picture seems even bleaker. Not only is their subjective experience all they have to go on, but their 'inner life' is as liable to error as a sentence. Hope and faith might be in abundance, but don't necessarily lead one to 'Truth'.

Logicians use extremely simple sentences to analyse, those with a subject and a predicate. As an act of communication, it requires the *understanding* of its readers. A reader must know what each word refers to. If a proposition is simple enough, it is possible to call it 'true' (provided it remains reducible to a logical proposition, and without the context or intonation of a speech act where its meaning might become too complex for a straightforward true/false evaluation).

But religious/artistic language works quite differently. It points, suggests, hints, evokes, but cannot by its very nature pin down. It is an act of communication between one *imagination* and another.

We use both kinds of language, even small children, and both kinds of language depend on grammar to make sense.

There are rules to learn. Chomsky famously argued that these structures were innate: almost all languages have nouns, verbs and adjectives. It's true: epigenetics suggests that the behaviour of previous generations has an effect on the present generation, and the fact that our ancestors used language before us might well make it *biologically* easier to pick up a language. But if you imagine our ancestors *discovering* how to use language – rather than *inventing* a language, (as I did as a child, complete with dictionary and a list of irregular verbs), the nature of language as first and foremost a mode of communication will be obvious. It doesn't fit into the neat tramlines of the logicians, yet its ambition is nonetheless to refer to the world outside the self and communicate it to others. And if we know this, the need for grammar becomes obvious. Grammar is like a grid that turns mere sounds into stable points of reference for all those who use it. So we need nouns, adjectives, verbs and the rest because this is what human beings need and want to talk about: we name things about us, to save us the time of pointing; we commend or disapprove of activities, describing them as 'good' or 'bad' or 'dangerous'. Thumbs up, thumbs down, yes, no, 'understood', 'I know', the nod or shake of the head, this, that, the noises we make of commendation or anger: a common language *works* in a society because it *evolves* in that society, and as it becomes more complex is *taught* in that society. A complex language is a short cut to a civilization, where questions are asked, and new 'knowledge' stored by writing, and added to at a rate impossible in a primitive society.

Yet even in a primitive society, words are more complex than they seem at first sight. A child, or even a dog (if they had the words) might take issue with the Wittgenstein of the *Tractatus* complaining that words are not simply pictorial. When a toddler says the word 'milk' his meaning includes the desire to drink milk; when I say the word 'walk' to my dog, he has never complained that 'walk' is not a thing to which any of us can point, but an idea which lends itself to a verb far more than a noun. There is no happy latching on of word to reality.

The academic way language is taught – and certainly, second languages are taught in school – should not betray the experience of it, and the fact that the experience is a *primary* one. The easy way young children use tenses of verbs show they have already understood the notion of *time* – soon, tomorrow, yesterday, and I have always thought it a tragedy that I can't explain the meaning of these words to my dog, who waits expectantly all day long for the magic word 'walk'. He comes to see me with his lead in his mouth to remind me of its pleasures, quite sure that I have simply forgotten them.

As we get older we discover these two functions of language: the language that pins down, and the language that paints. Both kinds work, but in different ways, and sometimes they work simultaneously, more often than we would think. Rowan Williams makes the point in his book *Being Human* that we have literally become 'narrow minded' in our high estimation of the skill-set of the left-hand, logical side of the brain, and relative scorn of the right-hand side of the brain, which gives us a sense of an horizon.

When we use the word 'imagination', for example, we immediately think of fanciful people who have little hold on 'reality'. However, as the word suggests, it means to hold an 'image' of something within your mind. We are suspicious because private mental images are subjective, and the idea is that 'Truth' is going to be something like 'pure objectivity' – an objectivity, no less, which can be verified. But we use mental images all the time, which are both private and incommunicable. When we wonder how a particular friend is getting on in New York, we often miss out language altogether, conjuring up an essence or an image both of the friend and of the city. In fact, the only thing we know beyond doubt is that we have a mental life. When Descartes pronounced, 'cogito, ergo sum' he didn't even presume that his mere 'thinking' meant that he had a body. Our own subjectivity is probably the only thing of which we are absolutely certain, and even that we cannot prove to anyone else.

Yet, despite our poor estimation of imagination, we unwittingly use it in everyday perception. The right-hand side of our brain is informing us that the tree we are looking at has a back to it. We don't actually *see* the back, and certainly can't *prove* that it has a back, but subliminally we imagine the tree as an entire entity because, and only because, *we have experience of trees.*

The experience of trees is prior to forming a concept of 'tree'. Trees existed before 'trees' existed, and will probably go on existing after the death of the last person who says 'tree'. My experience of a particular tree does not depend on my understanding the word 'tree', but if I wish to communicate that experience to a friend, out of sight of the tree (and cannot simply point at it) I will need to know how to use the universal 'tree', and the person to whom I say the word 'tree' will share that knowledge.

But the word 'tree' is going to get me so far and no more. Perhaps I am able to use the word 'oak' accurately, and my friend can too, and that will mean she has a better idea of what I'm talking about. Or I might mention the colour and shape of the leaves, the roughness and thickness of the bark. But I will fail to get my experience of the tree across, unless I am a practised nature writer or a poet. A poet uses words like brush strokes, and creates an image like an artist. The endeavour is entirely different: one imagination addressing another, with words as cues, gliding you into meaning line by line. As I am not a poet, my experience of a particular tree remains infuriatingly ineffable.

But what I am quite certain of is this: experience is ontologically prior to trying to talk about it. I am remembering a sight which was real, and which concerned stuff out there in the world, even if I don't have the words to describe it.

Richard Rorty will have a problem with this, as well as any who believe in the hermeneutic circle of knowledge – that sentences are inter-referential and ultimately controlled by those in power, which force our thinking down tramlines which benefit them. Interestingly, these philosophers use circular arguments to prove their point. Rorty's goes like this:

> Truth is a property of sentences. Sentences are dependent for their existence on vocabularies, and since vocabularies are made by human beings, so are truths.[122]

Yet look again at his argument. 'Truth is a property of sentences' – what does he mean by that? If he means simply, that we call some sentences 'true' in a pragmatic, social way, but they don't actually represent reality in any meaningful way, then indeed, Rorty can make his circular argument, and we can't escape it. Even Wittgenstein threw the baby out with the bathwater in his *Investigations*. If language doesn't represent reality in a properly connecting way, if there is no *hors-texte*, as Derrida says, if language is nothing but a game with its own rules, if language isn't Truth-seeking, indeed why bother with it? Why not just get along with other people, with the rest of our herd?

At the end of the *Tractatus*, Wittgenstein tells us poetically, 'whereof we cannot speak, thereof we must be silent.' Because only language which latches perfectly onto reality can be considered true, and he doesn't want to include any second-rate sentences to spoil his pictorial theory of truth. Yet if we human beings had followed his advice there would be neither literature nor scripture. That's what similes and metaphors and countless other literary devices are for: they try to reach something that can't be said. The first piece of advice given to the creative writing student is 'show, don't tell.' Or, 'paint a picture, don't speak in propositions'. Notice, the very opposite advice one would give to an academic scientist or historian.

At the end of his book on Wittgenstein, talking about the 'tension' between his two books, the philosopher David Pears writes:

> The linguistic naturalism by itself would have been a dreary kind of philosophy done under a low and leaden sky. The resistance to science by itself might have led to almost any kind of nonsense. But together they produced something truly great.[123]

And Pears is right, we need both approaches. Just because language often fails, just because people misunderstand each other so often, and read books and poetry in very different ways, doesn't mean that we should reduce its remit. No, language doesn't latch onto reality terribly well, but it can do, most particularly the language of mathematics which has proved itself again and again by making predictions about reality which have only recently been proved by the particle accelerator at Cern. We need to re-learn our trust in language, but wisely, aware of how it can inform us but also dupe us.

A short time ago a friend and I went to visit her distant cousin, who told us a story about his parents. He told it with a wry smile, and let us, his audience, fill in the gaps. This is what he told us, using simple propositions, all of which might be deemed 'true' in so far as they corresponded with facts that were known by the family and indeed could be verified. They were therefore, 'meaningful'.

My parents had an unhappy marriage.

They divorced when I was ten.

My father lived abroad for fifty years.

I lived with my mother in West Sussex, until I left home.

My father returned when he thought he was getting dementia.

My mother got dementia.

They ended up in the same residential care home.

Now they are rarely apart, and want to marry.

On the way home I enthused to my friend about her cousin's story. It was romantic, I said. Somehow they must have remembered their love for each other all that time ago. My friend was shocked. These two people had an illness that had obliterated their history and identity. They didn't know what they were doing.

I write fiction, and my friend writes non-fiction. We both think of ourselves as truth-loving. We would both hate to think we were deceiving ourselves. Yet one of us is: who?

Some linguistic philosophers might define 'truth' as the sum of true statements. This is true *and* this is true *and* this is true, and so on *ad infinitum* – and all the propositions there isn't time to express. And one can see how, linguistically at least, this works. The story above was told in eight 'true' statements, and it might be that if we could tell the story in a million 'true' statements we might understand the 'true' story, which my friend and I would agree on. I don't know, for example, whether the couple ever loved each other for a day, and the 'true' statements might help me assess that.

However I didn't use the analytic, linguistic part of my brain to reach the conclusion I did to judge whether the story was indeed a romantic one, or me projecting 'romance' onto it because *I* am a romantic. In fact, I was so taken with the story, I didn't really care whether it was literally true or not: if I had read it as a subtle short story, for example – subtle, because too much sentiment would have been cliché and I would have discarded it out of hand. But freshly told, it would make a charming one.

Human beings are hungry for meaning. Not only do we like love stories, but we like art and music. We find meaning both in our own creative activities, and in the creative activities of others, activities which circumvent the need for language altogether. But because these activities cannot be held down, scrutinized, reduced to statements, philosophy has tended to dismiss them as being peripheral. Yet they are central to the human condition. And the reason why they work on us so well is that they are activities that look toward a horizon, breaking down each new horizon even as it approaches. If it actually succeeded in reaching a horizon, it would thereby achieve closure and lose its power. It might even be reducible to statements, and die. Language categorises, that's how it works, how it communicates, how it pins down. But when you pin down, you kill. Here is the paradox, by making sure that a statement is watertight and thereby 'true', you lose sight of any larger conception of Truth, which is always unbounded. The hermetically sealed statement becomes an atom of the hermeneutically sealed circle of knowledge: it can't breathe. It doesn't go anywhere but falls back on itself, making new knowledge, and indeed science itself, a chimæra.

Societies, likewise, need to have horizons that they don't reach and they cannot know. Meaning needs space. Atheists often dismiss 'God' as a 'God of the gaps'. Zeus sends down his thunderbolts, but once we know that thunder is caused by the rapid heating of air by lightning, then Zeus has one less role. Our ancestors believed that plagues might be a sign of God's wrath, but now we understand more about the transmission of diseases, God's power is further diminished. The theory goes, that when we have filled all these gaps with scientific knowledge, there won't be any need of God and we will all come to our senses.

Yet imagine a society in which all was known. As an undergraduate, I was forever designing utopias. I didn't think of them as specifically communist, but one can scarcely say, 'It would be good if the ten percent at the bottom of the income scale are too poor to buy food, and often have to do without.' Ditto with all the goods of life: education, health and so on. I designed perfect houses and perfect streets in perfect towns, and was quite pleased with myself until I gave myself the option of actually living there. So the problem became more philosophical than political: why would I rather be dead than live in such a place?

Some years later I found the answer in a book, *Social and Biological Roles of Language* by Richard Totman. He writes:

> Imagine a society whose members are so socially harmonious as to have reached complete agreement over the rules of conduct. They are continually in unanimous accord over matters of convention, belief, morality, style, and so on. In such an 'ideal' society there would be no scope for choice and no role for justification because nothing would ever be in dispute and no alternative ways of acting would ever present themselves. People would conduct themselves like – indeed would effectively *be* – automata.[124]

The German philosopher Wilhelm von Humboldt said much the same thing at the end of the eighteenth century:

Whatever does not spring from a man's free choice, or is only the result of instruction and guidance, does not enter into his very being, but still remains alien to his true nature; he does not perform it with truly human energies, but merely with mechanical exactness.[125]

Making sense of our world, filling all the gaps that were once 'God', kills the best part in us, 'our true nature', which is both unbounded and loves unboundedness. We are drawn to mystery, tales of miracles, ghosts, the supernatural, tales that are 'strange but true'. They quicken the pulse, make us feel alert and alive. Conversely, a life feels 'meaningless' when all is explained, when each day is as predictable as the previous one. The unknown is a psychological imperative.

What I neglected to build in my Utopia was a church, not a church where all is sorted, sifted and understood, and transmitted as 'facts', as 'certainty', but a place of unknowing, a place to recognize that the asking of the question is more important than the answering of it. This is where our spiritual life resides. Paradoxically, we find our peace here. 'Be still and know I am God', says the psalmist. The words are so powerful, yet we have no idea what they mean: they take us somewhere, they do their work. And if we did know, when the yearning is over, when there is closure, the spirit recedes.

I use the word 'know' – and I'm sure the psalmist did too – in the broadest possible sense. 'Know' is just a word, translated, I'm sure, into every human language, but the various meanings a particular society gives it might be so different as to be incommensurate. In fact, our own two meanings were famously pointed out by Russell: 'knowledge by acquaintance' and 'knowledge by description' – or the French words, *connaitre* and *savoir* – and at first seem to have no overlap. Knowing something or someone by acquaintance requires *no* language, to begin with. Social scientists might be up in arms about this, believing that a mental idea requires a concept, and a concept requires a word, which is a social phenomenon. My dog, however, tells me they're quite wrong: he knows more with his nose than he can say.

What is it to know a person by acquaintance? Some people are better at this kind of 'knowing' than others. My dog happens to be very good at it: not only does he recognize the neighbours who will hand him titbits, but he knows intuitively which of them like dogs and which of them don't. 'Intuitively' means he has had many experiences over his lifetime which he will have forgotten about, and certainly doesn't 'verbalise', but the sum of it is that he *recognizes* the dog-lovers, and wags his tail when he sees them walking up the road towards him.

Human beings intuit in just the same way. In fact, one might learn 500 facts about a person, but still not 'know' that person in any significant sense. Doubtless fans of pop stars know many such facts. Yet when you meet someone face to face, and spend an evening with them, you pick up clues as to who and how they are which have nothing to do with language or knowing a range of true facts. The creative writer, who shows without telling, describes these clues to her readers – the posture, the facial expressions, and what was said – and not the *content* of what was said, but rather the fact that the character chose one thing to say ahead of another. 'The geraniums are looking fine this year' takes on a different meaning if the character is speaking a) as a keen gardener in a friend's garden or b) on the day of his mother's death. In a) there is nothing more to be said. In b) there is a huge amount more to be said, possibly a whole novel's worth.

Yet the modern West prefers facts, we want knowledge and facts to be bedfellows, and 'Truth' to be the sum of facts. A dog wagging his tail; a literary effect – am I being *serious?*

The irony is that it was our *language* which thrust facts and knowledge together in the first place. We gave such and such a meaning to the word 'knowledge' and then tried to fit it all in, like a swollen foot into a shoe. But facts are as vulnerable and as liable to error as our 'knowledge' of people. I might say, 'I know that the battle of Waterloo took place in 1066' and then records might throw that 'fact' into doubt. We humans depend on experts to give us the facts, and then we say we 'know' them. But we don't really. We have just been well trained in facts, facts which are easy to communicate because they have a shape of a proposition which can be analysed logically. But going back to the perfect society, where we are 'automata', and 'alien' to our 'true nature' what do we really *know* about anything? We have been trained, and led are merry dance. We are like those people in Plato's Cave who see only shadows, who don't realise there is a world out there with sunlight. We are like Truman in the film *The Truman Show,* who doesn't realise he is starring in his own TV show until he breaks through the screen which is the backdrop of the set. True knowing requires going back to the primary, non-linguistic experience; authenticity requires beginning afresh, in Socrates' words, knowing only that you know nothing.

Pure subjectivity, I would argue (with Descartes), is the first building block of knowledge. But we are social beings. In our subjectivity, we remain *unknown*, which is both lonely and painful. We reach out to others with gestures and with language, but language, as I have suggested, will only get us half way there, it's the sorting-house between one subjectivity and another, which is why we want art, which is why we want religion. We crave the spaces in between words, we crave their lack of certainty because then *anything* is possible.

The relationship between a true statement and Truth is made clear by the way in which we 'know' them. Only the statement is verifiable, and when it's verified, it becomes 'true'. But 'Truth' of the second kind is only recognized, and literally, ineffable. It is 'what is out there' and unpolluted, unfiltered by language. Derrida calls it *tout autre*. I call it, following others, the sublime. Language is a grid that holds things in place with concepts and grammar, but it is also, literally, *artificial,* as in, 'made by skill'. It's the project of human beings, the vehicle by which we transmit what we call 'knowledge'. We have to escape it, in order to return to it with new eyes.

Both in language and experience we come to know via an understanding of opposites. We learn 'hot' at the same time as 'cold', 'tidy' at the same time as 'untidy'. Psychologically, also, we learn about our freedom when we experience our unfreedom. When we are shocked out of our self-conscious selves, we return to find ourselves more conscious than ever. We learn how much we love someone when they are no longer there.

In the objective world, we come to know by means of a dialectic, a conversation, an argument. In the subjective world, there is also a dialectic, between free will and surrender. But there is a further dialectic: that between the subjective experience and the objective 'fact'.

I set out to show how the meaning in a sentence and 'facts' are analogous to the meaning of a life. Both require what is real, what is out there and what is ontologically prior, to break in. 'Truth' in the bigger sense needs both: it is what happens when time collides against the eternal.

The natural historian looks at a tree in a different way from the artist. His ideal account of it would be that of the photographer, capturing exactly the nature of the bark and leaves, in order to compare and contrast it with other trees. The historian will think in the same way, wanting to record events systematically and with no premature interpretation, if any. But the artist, the writer, wants to capture the *essence* of the whole, the universal aspect of it, its possible meanings, its timelessness. The artist interprets, and wants to share his interpretation with others.

There is no winner here. If there is such a thing as truth, it needs both approaches, both ways of looking. The universal, the timeless, is unreachable without the particular informing it. The particular without the universal is little more than data. Human beings are meaning-seeking animals; we are hungry for it. But finding that meaning, that ultimate truth, that Logos is a solitary task.

Fear and Longing

A Symposium

Overture

This symposium arose out of a video conference (it took place during the Covid-19 lockdown) between the artist John B. Harris (**JH**), wordsmith Olivia Fane (**OF**) and editor Keith Sutherland. Keith had been struck by a paragraph from a theology thesis Olivia had written some time ago:

> Kant is describing the rapid alternation of fear and longing, attraction and repulsion. For Kant, this is no mere, pleasant contemplation of the sublime. The sublime rests precariously on the edge of an abyss, and we do not know what we will find.

Keith recalled that John (who he had known for over half a century) had a painting entitled 'Fear and Longing' that he thought might make a suitable cover for an amended version of the thesis (the first essay in this volume). Out of this has grown a remarkable syzygy between images and words, intimation and explication, leading to the following conversation (loosely reconstructed along the lines of a Platonic dialogue).

OF: I think Kant is right when he suggests in his *Critique of Judgment* that the way we use the adjective sublime is wrong. We should not be calling a sunset or a mountain view sublime, as sublimity does not refer to the objects themselves but to our experience of them. We are shaken out of the commonplace by astonishment, by awe, and in Burke's description of 'sheer terror' we leave our everyday selves behind and look afresh. It's a moment of losing self-consciousness – literally losing our sense of self and immersing ourselves in what we do not know. It's a moment of surrender.

JH: Yes absolutely. I think that the experience of the sublime really does preclude the sense of personality in the sense that the social self is really a construct that only gets in the way of truth and what we're really talking about is a perception of that which is stripped of all those characteristics with which we associate our self.

OF: I find it an enormous relief to be stripped of self. I love all activities that strip away the sense of being an 'I'. It is exhausting being an 'I' and I think that's why all human beings are attracted to the sublime, because that sense of responsibility – having to decide what to do next – is taken from us.

JH: The only reservation I have about that is the concept of the 'I' and what we refer to when we talk about it. There is a vast range of understanding that goes from the commonly understood sense of ego – they're doing this, I'm doing that and so on – and a wider and less tangible concept, which is one of *presence* which doesn't have a location or identity attached to it. There are moments in people's lives when the perception of the social I is diminished to such a degree that it allows a dim perception of something that lies beyond that social self – a sense of the self beyond.

OF: I think that's why I loved your painting on the front of this book. There's a door and then there's Beyond the door (I call it a door but you might not have conceived of it as a door – it's a rectangular dark space). You do not know what is beyond it and as soon as I saw it I recalled two paintings in my sitting room at home. One is called 'The handle of the door' and the other is called 'There is a room to which there is no key' (a verse from the *Rubaiyat* of Omah Khayyam). As soon as I saw your own painting I thought, 'Aha, I've been here before, and evidently John has too. How might our experiences compare?' For myself, I find it irresistible both to knock on it and to open it rather aggressively – too aggressively you might say – and see what happens next.

Why I love that door is occasionally I get tired of being a creature of time and cultural space – the responsibility, the family, the things that I have to do – all the 'normal' stuff. Sometimes I just want to escape and to go to a place where paradoxically I can simultaneously leave myself far behind for a sensation which is emptier, truer and more alert. There's a phrase in the Christian liturgy – 'lift up your hearts', and that's how it feels, I literally feel heightened. And here's another paradox: I make myself so vulnerable, and yet have absolute faith that all will be well – which takes us right back to fear and longing. But John, you painted a picture and gave it the same title. What is beyond that dark rectangular shape that I call a door? Can you describe the feeling which motivated you?

JH: In my case it's a little bit more complicated because I don't see it as a door – in fact I see it as a space of unknowing. The experience that generated it was entirely traumatic – it was one of plunging into a space in which the ego could not survive. There was absolutely no question of being able to go through that door and remain as a person and there was no question of return – it's a one-way ticket. The point about that is that naturally the one that we think of as ourselves is totally terrified of it. I remember it better than most of the experiences in my life – because it impinges on everything. I used to suffer a lot from migraines – I was at art college and I had this terrible migraine and I went to lie on my bed feeling sick as a dog. I lay back in the bed and was just trying to deal with this sense of all-encompassing pain and something totally unexpected occurred which initially excited me enormously because I've always been interested in experiences that lie beyond the normal domain. What happened was my vision went black and then this vast moon just rose up. It was absolutely huge and there was nothing else in my perception – of me or anything else. I was so shocked, as it was the moon that I knew well because I've always been interested in astronomy so I could see all the craters and I just couldn't believe the intensity of the reality of it. I was still thinking at this point perfectly clearly and it was replaced by an image of galaxies and I was watching this vast galaxy turn. Now I just happened to know that a galaxy takes at least 200 million years to rotate around its axis on average! I was just so overwhelmed that I just couldn't believe it, but then something changed that went dark and that was replaced by the most awful sense of falling into a black hole. There's no other way to describe it – I was being sucked into this infinitely deep black hole and I was falling backwards into it and realizing that this was my death. There was no doubt whatsoever that it was a sense of dying. I have no idea how long any of this lasted, but I felt myself falling and falling and falling and then something took over which was my history of myself and not wanting to lose it. The reason why I didn't want to lose it was because I had the feeling that I had travelled so far with that being and had managed to climb out of some unknowing and here I was falling back into that unknowing and I couldn't bear it. I couldn't bear the thought of erupting out of that with less than I had been before, and this was where the dying came in. I realized this is irrevocable, this is the end, this is it.

But I was so determined not to let that go – that little kernel of being that I knew to be me. I had no choice really. There was no question of choosing to let go or not choosing to let go. I was terrified – completely and utterly mindlessly terrified – and every part of me started to struggle to get out of the hole. And somehow it happened that I crawled out – this sense of drifting up, and somehow or other I managed to climb out of it. These descriptions are not really adequate to describe the feeling but I managed to climb out of it and then as I got to the point where I realized I was going to get out, this overwhelming sense of sadness came and it was the recognition that I had been *falling into home that was really me*, and that me was not John Harris, it was something ineffable, inexplicable.

OF: Yes, it's interesting that a lot of people fear death because they're frightened of losing that basic 'me'.

JH: That's why I call it a near-death experience. There's no way it could be any less than that. Ever since so much of my energy has been spent trying to regain that sense of home. But I know it's not in my power to invite it or to remove it.

OF: So have you had experiences like that again?

JH: There have been one or two things but they're not relevant in the sense that everything that happens this side of that 'well' is all changing anyway. You know all this [points to his body] will be gone in twenty years' time and that's absolutely fine because I know that it's nothing to do with me. This is why there is this sense of longing to be reunited with what *is* me.

OF: I had an equivalent experience when I was twenty-five. I was on a yacht for two days and nights in a force ten gale and I'd never even been on a yacht before. I have to show off here – I'm terribly good at surrendering, so I didn't even get the slightest bit of seasickness. I just gave myself over to the sea quite happily. And the sea was magnificent, it was so huge, and I thought gosh I might really possibly die. And when I looked at my life – I have a husband who I love, I have a child I love, I have a life I love, and yet death is sweeter still than that. It was so rough, the sails were taken down and we had to lie in our bunks, which were rather appropriately coffin-shaped. So I was lying there with my feet together in my coffin-shaped tomb feeling that's okay, this is absolutely fine, this is completely glorious to be here. And I had this great smile on my face, and it went on for forty-eight hours this storm. I mean can you relate to that?

JH: Absolutely, I wished I had been more mature in myself when I had my own experience of it, because the way you're describing it sounds so tempting – I might be dead but that's just fine, you know! What happens when you get confronted with that reality is that the furniture of one's being is shifted around the room. You'll never be quite the same again, but even more important and more significant I think is the attitude towards what you *are*. I had already, many years before this experience, adopted briefly the discipline of self-inquiry, which is a practice of meditation. It's not really meditation in the normal sense of the word but I had already turned my attention 180 degrees from the outward to the inward and had a very extraordinary shift of awareness as a result of it that had happened five years before. This completely changed everything before this event, but I was still not mature enough to benefit from the exposure to the well or what I would now call the 'maw of death'. It really is a grinder!

OF: And when you were back in the everyday world, did you have a sense of 'have I been singled out to do something great, am I supposed to tell everybody this?'

JH: No. I can see clearly that *everybody* has this in the background of their mind. The only thing is whether we shore up and build up defences against it or whether we open up to it. Now in your case I would have said that your maturity was such that you knew what was what. To be clear, by 'maturity' I mean a knowledge of the true state of affairs which we all of us subconsciously know but most of us don't accept, that the social construct is just that – it's just a construction.

OF: I don't know why more people don't accept that because it's pretty much staring us in the face.

JH: Yes, but we invest in it – we all, through the nature of our culture, invest in the story of our lives.

OF: I still teach Latin and Greek, and I enter from time to time this completely other realm where the mores are different but similar – the idea that luck, for example, might be some kind of goddess. You might not have been a classicist but you've invented an entire other world yourself in *The Rite of the Hidden Sun*. Although you are a painter you liken yourself to a Victorian explorer and try to piece together what that civilization was like. And that's exactly what I do when I enter my classical world and I think one of the things that strikes you is how random and contingent our culture is and how there is nothing more serious about it than a game of Monopoly, where you learn the rules and obey them if you're to succeed.

JH: Yes that is all in the realm of this side of the door and it is part of the storytelling that incarnate beings like to do – it's part of the joy of living that we have these constructs.

OF: One thing that struck me in that series of paintings is the absolutely terrifying rites of passage you make both the young men and the young women do in order to get to the temple. The young women have to balance precariously on this zigzag wall about six inches wide and first of all they have to achieve total equanimity before they're even allowed to do it. If you are totally relaxed and calm you can balance there and you can reach the top, but you have to risk everything and you have to know fear and master it in order to reach your destination. Meanwhile the young men have a totally different project – they swoop down on a parachute and hang over the core of the volcano. Their rite is also terrifying.

JH: Yes, this point is very pertinent to this whole debate, because I have noticed throughout my life that women don't need a lot of encouragement to let go. Generally speaking I think most women are very good at letting go, but with most men the nature of our culture is such that they don't want to and they need to be beaten around the head! On the one hand you have the serene situation of the girl who walks on this knife edge of a wall and the whole point is that her serenity and her equilibrium renders her competent for the rite. The rite is necessary in order to be able to benefit from the solitude and the sanctuary of the temple, but for the men it's an entirely different affair – they have to literally have their being wrested

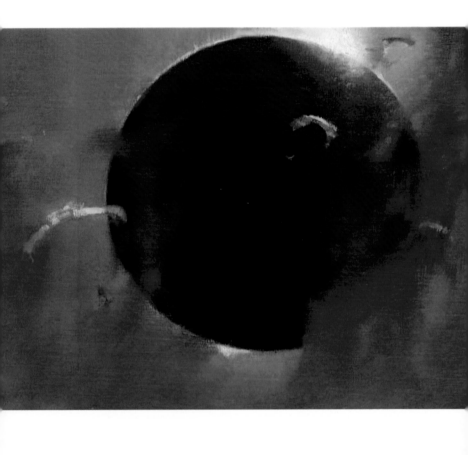

from them. This refers back to my experience, which was that I had no bloody choice! There wasn't any question of surrender, there was only being thrown into the pit and did I have the strength to climb out of it?

The irony of the whole affair is that if I had not had the strength to climb out of it, it might have been very different and rather wonderful, but that's a separate issue. From the point of view of the men, the idea was that I wanted to subject them to first of all taking the edge off their mentality and that was achieved by the vapours of the volcano, which produces a vast cocktail of chemicals, many of which could be profoundly narcotic. The Delphic Oracle was almost certainly placed over a chasm which exhaled some kind of volcanic vapour that gave the Priestess of Apollo the edge to have her visions. This was the first step of the rite.

So I imagined this boy, Cotl – incidentally it wasn't a rite before he did it, there always has to be a first time – there he was trying to find a way to get over the chasm that had filled up with lava in order to be able to get to the centre of the volcano and turn the valves on. So he launches himself off, having told his father: don't worry about me, I've already developed this hang-gliding skill. He is very confident and safe in his masculinity of being able to overcome something with his skill, which is dealing with the thermals and this canopy of silk. What he hadn't taken into account was the power of the volcano to disrupt his mind – through the narcotics or the chemistry of the vapours – so there he is, struggling with the mechanical problem of keeping afloat, and at the same time losing the very thing that gives him that ability to do it.

OF: Oh yes that's really interesting – control and lack of control.

JH: Exactly, so that's the centre of it, that's why I say men have to be beaten around their head. They have to do it accidentally – maybe I *needed* to have that migraine.

OF: In fact this question goes to the absolute centre of life – when to control it and when to surrender to it. When I sit down to write a novel I also have to beat myself up to get behind the computer screen – I'll do anything rather than settle down to the job. I begin very consciously and my will is on full steam ahead, and then suddenly about half a paragraph in I am lost and I am gone and then the rest of it takes care of itself. But in every aspect of life it has always seemed like this, even, say, catching mice in your house – there is the time to go all out to catch mice, and a time to say, well the mice are always going to find a way in so let's co-habit and make the most of it. The wisdom you get with living a long time is when to start controlling and when not.

Actually that's one of the feelings that I had about your painting. When you were talking about the project you did at NASA – *The Secret History of the Earth* – you said that you tried to mix the dust and the glue, but it was precarious, it didn't want to stick and so it was like a dialogue with the painting itself to see what it would let you do to it and then you suddenly recognized it as *good*, this is what I wanted to do. You

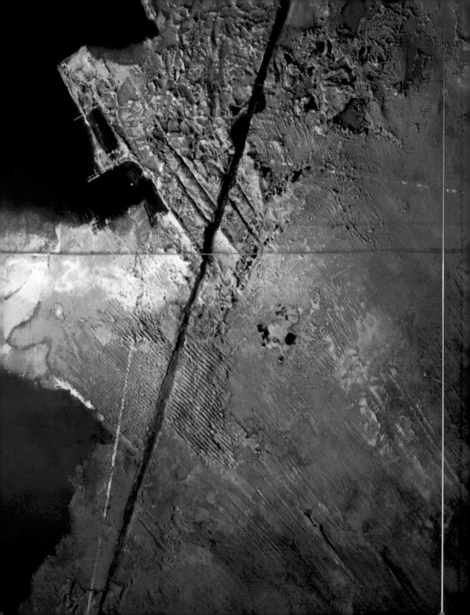

were saying to me earlier that it's the feeling that comes first, but for me as a novelist it is the concept which comes first – that's a good idea for a story. But for you it's the feeling and what's interesting is what are these feelings made of? What was exciting talking to you earlier is *Veda* and the *vasanas*, because I think they're really relevant to how you paint.

JH: Yes, they're relevant to how we all behave. The idea is that in the culture of the *Veda*, which goes back probably a good five thousand years, there was an entirely different emphasis to social life. It was the consequence of the inner, rather than the outer world being understood. In the Vedic culture they had developed the skills to understand the mechanism of experience before they knew about the subject matter of what they were experiencing. We don't really know very much about it, because it's an oral tradition and the time scales are very shady, but to the best of our knowledge what happened was around four or five thousand years ago there were a number of these people who had developed this introspective skill and the ability to remain conscious at a very subtle level where they could understand the mechanisms that govern our behaviour. They understood mostly that the body itself is a record of our behaviour and that imprinted into our biological system are all of the traces of the traumas and the joys and desires and all of these things that govern our behaviour. They called these embodied tendencies *vasanas*, (*logismoi* in the parlance of Athonite Christianity) and these tendencies determine to a large degree pretty much everything that we do. In fact I would go so far as to say that the social animal as we understand ourselves is almost entirely the consequence of our vasanas – these tendencies that are built into the biological system. So what they immediately applied themselves to, was to first of all perceive, study and observe how these vasanas operated in the world and, having done that, to *undermine* them because it was their opinion that the truth about our nature could only really be seen when the vasanas are to a large extent weakened and overcome. The interesting point about it is that the culture out of which the Vedas came enabled them to understand that they didn't need to get rid of the vasanas, they just had to be able to sidestep them.

OF: The next thing I want to ask you is to do with art history. Before the last hundred years in the history of modern painting the most important thing was what the artist saw – there is something real which is out there and it's the job of the artist to depict that reality and that reality is what takes precedence. In other words I'm going to be absolutely faithful to the image – I'm going to learn the skills to paint this tree, or this face or this hat as it is. And then photography comes along and suddenly it's not *what* the artist sees so much as what the *artist* sees. It's about *his* vision, it becomes individualistic and we get to focus on the names of artists. It matters if somebody is Picasso, as it's his vision that matters. I want to ask you which of those two kinds of artists you are – is it you the artist that matters or what you see that matters and what is exciting for me is that somehow you manage both to be entirely imaginative – this is your vision this is your imagination – and yet you know how to paint really well and you fit comfortably within the pre-modern tradition of representational art.

JH: This has always been a source of puzzlement to me because I didn't have a very clear idea about what kind of painter I wanted to be, it's just that I was motivated by feeling, and I did my best to describe that feeling in whatever shape or form I could. You've described very clearly a view of art ranging from the period of figurative and representational painting up through modern painting, but I don't recognize it as the way in which I went – either of them. I was lucky to have the tutorship of Mike Garton, a representational artist who was gifted not with a manner of painting but a way of seeing, and he effectively deconstructed my way of seeing so that I could learn to paint the way he saw. The way he saw was almost as a *tabula rasa*, where you don't see a plant, a vase, a table and a floor etc., what you see are the constructs of it in the shapes, the light, the shadows, the colour and so on as if you had no personality, as if you had no memory and as if you had no history of seeing. He taught me the building blocks of convincing reality.

Although Mike was famous amongst painters he was not featured in the media at all because his paintings weren't consciously cultural. When you look at all of the well-known modern painters they are all famous because of their contribution to culture. If you think of Picasso or Matisse, if you think of Frank Auerbach, or Francis Bacon, or Graham Sutherland, they were all contributors to the view of our culture. They became popular because they started a fashion, and the moment that they became well known it was a self-perpetuating monster which eventually produced this crippling celebrity culture we have now where everybody is desperate to achieve fame because they see it as a mechanism of capturing our culture (in the proprietary sense) instead of expressing their vision. It's the wrong way around as far as I was concerned and I quite early on consciously chose not to go to a London art college because it was dominated by the pop art culture and by the painters who wanted to be like Francis Bacon, or Lucien Freud.

OF: It makes me feel incredibly sad. I knew the art critic Tom Lubbock and I remember trying to promote my brother-in-law who I think is a fantastic artist and I said look couldn't you just write a piece about him in your newspaper? He looked at his work and said well these paintings are completely terrific but I can't for there's no hook — you have to have a line (note the angling metaphors), as people have to know what it is that they're supposed to be looking at.

JH: You've actually hit on one of the prime motivations that I had, which was a reaction against the peer group pressure to actually find a style that would cement my position in the echelons of art. This is completely misguided, so one of the main reasons why I came down to Exeter (where, in the late 1960s, respect for the artisanal tradition still survived) was to allow myself that context so that I could just be a painter. I didn't get a grant, as my parents didn't want me to go to art college and they said if you want to do this you do it on your own and consequently I went through art college completely broke. I just knew I had an ability, but I didn't know what I wanted to do with it – all I had was a heightened sense of the mystery of this . . .

OF: Oh the mystery of this! *Quiddity* – do you know this word?

JH: Yes I've heard that expression before and it's a lovely word and I think I know what it means without being able to explain it.

OF: It's the magic of *thisness*.

JH: That's great because that, I think, is the touchstone of real art – the sense of the mystery of what the hell is going on here? To my mind there is nothing more mysterious than the human being and there is nothing about the human being more mysterious than his or her *awareness*.

So without really thinking about all of that metaphysical stuff I just did what I could, which was to learn the craft of seeing and somehow or other through some agency that I have no control over, I gradually acquired the mechanisms of perception and practical application that enabled me to describe whatever it was that came into my mind.

OF: You remind me of an essay by the philosopher Anthony O'Hear in which he contrasts the real with the Real in the work of Chardin and Rothko. With Chardin we're

shown nice domestic items like spoons (the real with a small r),
or should art be about the big transcendent R (as with
Rothko)? This is the last paragraph from the essay:

> Against such a background the emptiness and perhaps the
> rhetoric of Rothko would be vindicated against the
> painstaking and human modesty of Chardin, and what
> Chardin presents to us as an all-too-fragile achievement will
> be swallowed up in the abyss of the divine. At the same
> time it is doubtless true that we come to see Chardin's
> achievement as the achievement it is just when we begin to
> understand that we are standing above an abyss cosmically
> speaking and that human domesticity and human
> perception rest on no secure foundation. In terms of my
> illustrative analogy then Rothko's real might be seen to
> serve as the background from which Chardin's reality and
> ours emerges and is perceived.[126]

So all is luminous on account of the transcendent.

JH: The sad thing is that Rothko died by his own hand.
The trouble is he didn't go far enough. Any Rothko painting
has this presence, but you have to stay with it and this is the
thing that I suspect that Rothko never learnt to do because he
was so overwhelmed by his Jewish culture. I may be wrong
about this as I really don't know very much about him, but
everything about his paintings tells me that that was his
problem – that he couldn't justify his journey to his own
culture and he saw the emptiness of the flattery. I didn't really

The Copper Cauldron, by Jean-Siméon Chardin

appreciate Rothko until I left art college and I went into the Rothko exhibition at the Tate – the one with the great maroon paintings. Ironically, they had been done for a restaurant – but they were astounding in the sense that they crossed the barriers of perception in a way that made them more audible than visible. They were in a very dim light and there was nothing else but they are really enormous and you're overwhelmed by the presence of the nine huge canvases. Up to that point fabulous, but then comes the decision of the individual or the observer as to what to do with that sense of presence. Personally I don't think that Rothko had the means culturally to let go of his vision of himself as an artist – I don't think he could deal with that experience. It's very sad. There must be in Greek mythology some god who gives, and on giving kills you?

OF: Whenever I've done any sort of performance at a literary festival and you give absolutely of yourself for an afternoon and you read from your book or you talk about yourself, there follows a kind of self hatred, for want of a better word. You want to be swallowed up by the earth, you hate yourself so. The first time this happened to me I remember thinking why do I feel like this? And it's because, I think, in public you present yourself as this ego, this *sorted* person, dressing for the role, speaking her speech like someone confident and professional, and somehow you manage to pass off that way. You almost persuade yourself you *are* that person and then you realize that you've been lying and you're a fraud.

JH: Yes I think it's quite a cogent reality. And what's the solution, if you're not going to commit suicide, you're not going to shoot yourself like either Van Gogh did or Rothko?

OF: You could become a monk, like Leonard Cohen?

JH: Well maybe. In fact I did the same thing when I was in my early twenties, but actually it doesn't work! The problem is you take your vasanas with you – there are thousands of monks out there who are carrying the burden of themselves around unfulfilled, because I think the ones who come out the other end happy are the ones who've lost themselves, and that is ultimately the only way for a monk to be. The whole point of monasticism is that you lose yourself.

OF: About four years ago I went to Dharamshala, the Dalai Lama's refuge in India. It was the least holy place that you could imagine – you saw all these monks going around with their mobile phones and they were the only people who looked well fed in the entire place. They did all these yogic exercises – weird press-ups and stuff – and when we tourists appeared they looked round like distracted schoolboys.

JH: The same thing applies in the guru circuit, you know. I had a lengthy experience of that in the early 1970s until I decided that it isn't the way at all. It was only relatively recently that I really understood the path that both Keith and I were initiated into (a very simple ancient technique, which involved Vedic sounds). It was a way of dealing with the material that you have to hand – the social construct of an individual riddled with vasanas (tendencies you come into life with and which accumulate during life) and how do you purify that without destroying the life. The skill of the Vedic tradition was they had this understanding of the effect of certain sounds upon the nervous system, which would, whatever your mental constructs, undermine the vasanas as they stood and rearrange them. I didn't know about this for years and years – I knew a lot about the Vedic culture as a result of being with Maharishi for a long time but that didn't really do it. I've done the TM practice for over half a century, and in that time there have been changes within this body-mind construct that have made it possible. But it's a very long slow process, and there are many others that are much faster, but will probably achieve havoc in the average human being (which is why the average human being doesn't normally do them).

OF: What I really like about your painting, and felt incredible empathy with is not just your love of the ruins of ancient civilization and the traces they leave, but in the video *The Secret History of the Earth* you talk about the earth rewriting itself. The paintings are not abstract – somebody might think they are at first sight – but then you notice these lines. I immediately thought of song lines, I immediately thought of human beings as soon as I saw them, because they placed human beings deeply in the earth and made the earth our home and the universe our home. I loved the revelation of history of place through shadows lying just under the soil, and the earth as a slate constantly drawn upon by time and by man and the moving of continents all leaving their trace. You saw this series of paintings as a visual poem about the earth and I have to say they made me love the earth and love my home.

Then I saw your next video and there were all these ruins. When I go to church or to a cathedral or to an old building of worship, I love that sense of going backwards in time and looking at the gravestones that I'm walking on and seeing 1430 or whatever. There's an archaeological procedure called LADAR (laser detection and ranging), that was used in our village, and they discovered that right by our church is a clump of something or other over which there is a yew tree. They discovered this hillock is very very old – in other words there was a community on that hill where our church is two or three thousand years ago. Every time I go to church I nod to say I'm pleased I know about you, I nod to the graves of all the people who've died there, and I nod to this ancient hillock that even preceded that. So these ruins really matter to me, in fact I own a book called *These Ruins Are Inhabited*, which is a great title and it's absolutely true that the ghosts of all those people who have ever lived there are still there. And I love again that sense of being so random in time that this just happens to be my second, it just happens to be now, but it could have been then, in fact it might have been then and now, who knows? And I love my own mortality; I love the fact that I will die, that my life would not be meaningful if I were not going to die.

JH: I absolutely concur with that. There's a Russian poet named Marina Tsvetaeva. I have a recording of her reading a poem that beseeches the reader to 'love me for I am going to

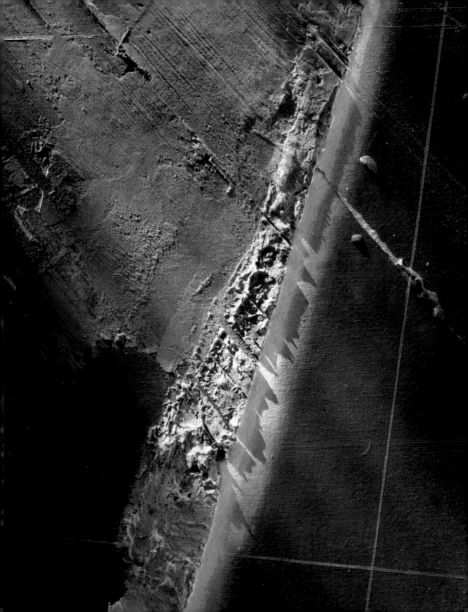

die and all of us are going to die'. It's a passionate plea to really pay attention to what is rather than what has been or what might be because that is why we're here.

OF: I say that to my husband every night and actually he says it back to me; we do talk about our own death continually as though we're just literally about to pop our clogs! Actually I hate the fact that one of us is going to die first, you know I don't want to be a widow – I mean I'm not going to be very good at it.

JH: So tell me – do you feel that you have the capacity for loneliness or are you happy to be alone?

OF: Well I said to my husband the other day actually – and he was very shocked by this – and I did say to him I feel so lonely at the moment, and in fact he took me in his arms and he said that that means he was failing, and what should we do now? So I immediately said let's read a bit of Schopenhauer together, or let's just go for a walk around the garden, or just sit next to me on the sofa, or do something with me but I remember it was very sudden and it suddenly came upon me.

I felt incredibly lonely in my early twenties and I was married at the time to somebody that I loved. I had a really good life and a good social life and we mixed with very interesting people whom I liked. What was interesting about feeling lonely is if you have a lot to say – and I have a lot to say, and you have a lot to say – well one person can't contain it all, which is why I spill out into writing my novels and you spill out into painting. There is too much to say to any one person or even a group of people and you would go mad if you did not say it. I wrote my first novel when I was twenty-seven and the first thing I noticed after I had written it was that sense of loneliness has left me.

JH: So this is obviously an issue of importance to you that somebody 'gets' you?

OF: When I wrote my first novel there was the sense that well somebody might read the whole thing and know me. The novel, *Landing on Clouds*, is about me being very lonely and my hero is a man who is desperately trying to stop being so lonely. His idea is to turn Mozart's *Prague Symphony* into all these colours that he feels. He listens to each few notes and he paints really carefully and it takes him twenty years to reach the end of the score and then he says, all that matters to me is that somebody one day will pick up this score and say 'actually that's just how I feel'. It's funny, after all these years I still identify with my hero. I just need an occasional 'yes', nothing more subtle than that. In my early twenties I would practically accost people I thought might understand me – 'Here I am! Can you relate to that? Do you feel that too?' I've finally learnt how to seem a little bit normal, and be quiet and listen. I've always had a yearning to know how it feels to be someone else, to wake up as another person. Sometimes I might ask a friend, 'What is it like to wake up as you in your bed? How long do you lie there before you get up? What do you think about?' I would dearly like to live one day as another person, with another mind, with another consciousness. But what about you and loneliness? Imagine a post-apocalyptic scene in which you are sitting in your cave, fully provisioned but entirely alone, what would be your mood?

JH: I would love to be able to say some of the things that you've said, but I can't – the reason being that I've always felt almost like a solipsist – I've always felt completely alone, but not lonely. I went to see the film *The Martian* quite recently. It was a film about a guy (Matt Damon) who's stranded on Mars and it's very realistically done. But at no point in the entire film – which was about two and a half hours long – did the director Ridley Scott consider the interior mindset of this guy. It was a very successful film and it was very good, but I kept thinking to myself this is just ridiculous – if I were stranded 200,000,000 miles away from earth on a planet with no living creature whatsoever, where the sun would rise and fall on a landscape that knew nothing of life at all and I was there to watch it, how would I feel and the first feeling that came across while I was watching this film was that this film is not addressing the central reality of his condition at all!

That's a preface to what I was going to say and I would have said that ten or twenty years ago I would have probably given a different answer to the one I have now, because I needed an audience for what I did. I needed an eye to see the pictures I've made other than my own. That no longer is quite the case for me – I can't really tell you why, except that the reality of being itself seems sufficient and that actually the entire world is contained inside the recognition that all of life, all of the thoughts that humans could ever have and so on, are there for a being that might want them but the being that observes doesn't need them.

OF: Why I mentioned that particular image is I've often wondered about myself in that cave and why I asked it particularly of you is because my feeling was about communion with the transcendent, about whether that communion would be sufficient to keep our sanity.

JH: Well, according to what we might call the 'Advaita perspective' you wouldn't have any mind to have sanity with, that's the rub of it. Advaita is the philosophy of non-duality in which it is purported that there is nothing other than the ground of being and that all of this 'stuff' is just a miasma that is being thrown up by a dreaming god. Our waking dream is a state of consciousness that doesn't actually reflect reality, which is undifferentiated radiant non-active being.

OF: What I quite liked about that idea was the other way round – if all things are equal, if the visible is equal to invisible, then also the invisible is real. In Plato's philosophy the forms are the reality, everything else is illusory, in that you're in the cave and you only see the shadows, or the reflection of the shadows.

JH: I remember the metaphor from reading it a long time ago, and it works up to a certain point and then it's a bit dicey because there's nothing to cast the silhouette on the wall, but that's another issue. The point about Advaita that I find particularly persuasive is that there are these two sides to everything – there is the changing side and there is the unchanging side – and by definition anything which doesn't change can be described as the truth, whereas that which changes cannot be described as the truth because it is never the same. We live in a world that is permanently changing, everything is in motion, nothing stays the same so nothing is true.

OF: Well everything in this is very Heraclitus – you can never step into the same river and yet the river exists, the ground of being exists . . .

JH: Exactly, and that's the sort of contrast between the changing and the unchanging. I may be wrong, but I think that the sum total of the Vedic knowledge that we've talked about in the past is the recognition of that polarity, but actually that polarity is itself merely a dream, and there is ultimately only the existence of unchangingness.

Endnotes

The Other Shore

[1] Shaw (2006), p.119
[2] Shaw, p.118
[3] Caputo (2001), p.126
[4] Caputo, p.115
[5] Caputo, p.127
[6] Longinus, trans. D.A. Russell (1965), p.1
[7] Longinus, p.2
[8] Longinus, p.9
[9] Burke (1990), p.1
[10] Burke, p.5
[11] Burke, p.5
[12] Burke, p.53
[13] Burke, p.53
[14] Burke, p.55
[15] Scruton (1996), p.311
[16] Burke, pp.56-57
[17] Burke, p.58
[18] Burke, p.67
[19] Kant (2003), trans. John T. Goldthwait, p.51
[20] Kant (2003), p.60
[21] Crowther (1989), pp. 20-21
[22] Kant (1955), trans. H.Paton, p.68
[23] Crowther (1989), pp.20-21
[24] Kant (1953), trans. James Creed Meredith, p. 15
[25] Kant (1953), p.18
[26] Crockett (2001), p.40
[27] Kant (1953), p. 90
[28] Kant (1953), p.91
[29] Kant (1953), p.91
[30] Kant (1953), p.91

[31] Kant (1953), p.92
[32] Lyotard (1991), p.123
[33] Lyotard, p.128
[34] Kant (1953), p.96
[35] Kant (1953), p.100
[36] Kant (1953), p.97-98
[37] Kant (1953), pp. 102-103
[38] Kant (1953), p.103
[39] Kant (1953), pp. 104-5
[40] Kant (1953), p.106
[41] Kant (1953), p. 110
[42] Kant (1953), p.127
[43] Kant (1953), p.179
[44] Kant (1953), pp.158-159
[45] Kant (1953), p.107
[46] Virgil, *Aeneid* Book vi, l.314 (1994) p. 528
[47] Frost (1972) p.145
[48] Lawson (2001), p.xxxii
[49] Wittgenstein in Lawson (2001), p.xxxii
[50] Lawson, p.xxxiii
[51] Lawson, p.xxxvii
[52] Lawson, p. xxxviii
[53] Lawson, p.239
[54] Lawson, p.240
[55] Lawson, p.240
[56] Lawson, p.240
[57] Brummer (1981) p.171
[58] Brummer (1981) pp. 174-175
[59] Brummer (1981) pp. 179-180
[60] Monti (2002), p.118
[61] Monti (2003), p.13
[62] Polanyi in Monti (2003), p.14
[63] Monti (2003), p.14
[64] Monti (2003), p.16
[65] Monti (2003), p.17
[66] Steiner, in Monti (2003), p.3

[67] Steiner, in Monti (2003), p.3.
[68] Monti (2003), p.44
[69] Lawson, p.133
[70] Lawson, p.133
[71] Lawson, p 134
[72] Lawson, p.134
[73] Lawson, p.228
[74] Lawson, pp.228-9
[75] Lawson, p.229
[76] Lawson, p.219
[77] Lawson, pp.196-197
[78] Burnham (2000), pp. 153-154
[79] Pillow (2003), p.6
[80] Pillow, p.6
[81] Pillow. p.69
[82] Pillow, p.69
[83] Pillow, p.69
[84] Kant (1953), p. 92
[85] Gilbert-Rolfe (1999), p. 45
[86] Clewis (2009), p.79
[87] Clewis, p.22
[88] Kant (1953) p.118
[89] Kant (1953) p.91
[90] Kant (1953) p.92
[91] Kant (1953), p.115
[92] Ades, Cox and Hopkins (1999) p.146
[93] Derrida in Monti (2003)p.3
[94] Monti (2003), p.3
[95] Gellner (1992), p.42
[96] Cupitt (1998), p. 95
[97] Caputo (2001), p. 128
[98] Caputo, p.129
[99] Blond (ed.) (1998), p. 259
[100] Hart in Blond (ed.) (1998), p.261
[101] Meister Eckhart trans. C de B Evans 1923 p.211
[102] Marion (1999), p.21

[103] Caputo (1999), p. 187

[104] Lawson, pp. 196-7

[105] Caputo (1999), p. 185-186

[106] Marion in God, The Gift and Post-Modernism p. 25

[107] Marion, in God, The Gift and Post-Modernism p.26

[108] Marion, p.26

[109] Marion, p.27

[110] Marion, in God,the Gift and Post-Modernism p.30

[111] Marion, p.43

[112] Eckhart (1981), pp. 183-184

[113] Eckhart in McGinn (2001), p.46

[114] Howell (2010), p.37

[115] Howell,p.38

[116] Caputo (1999), p.4

[117] Crockett (2001), p. 100

[118] Crockett, p.102

[119] Crockett, p.102

[120] Crockett, p.103

[121] Crockett, p.112

A Short Essay On Truth

[122] Rorty (1989), p. 21

[123] Pears (1971), pp. 183-4

[124] Totman (1985)

[125] von Humboldt (1993)

Fear and Longing

[126] O'Hear (2008), p. 86

Bibliography

Ades, Cox and Hopkins (1999) *Marcel Duchamp*, Thames and Hudson Ltd. London

Blond, Phillip (ed.) (1998), *Post-Secular Philosophy*, Routledge: London

Brummer, Vincent (1981), *Theology and Philosophical Inquiry; An Introduction*, Macmillan: London

Burke, Edmund (1990), *A Philosophical Enquiry into the Origin of our Ideas of the Sublime and Beautiful*, Oxford University Press: Oxford

Burnham, Douglas (2000), *An Introduction to Kant's Critique of Judgement*, Edinburgh University Press: Edinburgh

Caputo, John (1999) 'Apostles of the Impossible,' in Caputo and Scanlon (eds.), *God, the Gift and Postmodernism*, Indiana University Press: Indiana

Caputo, John (2001), *On Religion*, Routledge: London

Clewis, Robert (2009), *The Kantian Sublime and the Revelation of Freedom*, Cambridge University Press: Cambridge

Crockett, Clayton (2001), *Theology of the Sublime*, Routledge: London

Crowther, Paul (1989), *The Kantian Sublime*, Oxford University Press: Oxford

Cupitt, Don (1998), *Mysticism after Modernity*, Blackwell: Oxford

Eckhart, Meister (1991) trans. M.O'C. Walshe, *Sermons and Treaties*, Vol.1, Element Books: Boston

Frost, Robert (1972), *Poetry and Prose*, Holt, Rinehart and Winston: New York

Howell, Edward (2010), 'Meister Eckhart's Spirituality of Creation as Nothing' in *The Eckhart Review*